11+ Vocabulary
© Jane Armstrong, 2019

All rights reserved. No part of this book may be reproduced or transmitted in any form or by any means without written permission of the author.

Published : Jane Armstrong, 2019

Please read the following carefully before you begin the tests:

- Each test should take no more than 10 minutes. It is wise to get into the habit of limiting the time you spend on each test. This is good preparation for the real thing.

- Read the title of the question carefully. Many points have been lost by a child mistaking a request for antonyms rather than synonyms for example.

- Use each question as an opportunity to broaden your vocabulary. Once you have completed a test make a note of any words you may not have heard of before and look them up online or in a dictionary. Also find out if they have an antonym or a synonym.

- Good luck and have fun. You will learn more and want to continue learning if you are enjoying yourself.

Test 1

1. Antonyms

Select the word from the list that has the most opposite meaning to the word in **bold**.

Background	upbringing	culture	actions	foreground	behind
Commend	criticise	approve	hail	view	challenge
Rear	cultivate	train	fore	challenge	rise
Everyday	mundane	regular	automatic	rare	common
Muddled	mess	confuse	organised	dry	chaos

2. Fill in the missing words

Choose the most appropriate word from the list available to complete the following passage. One of the words will not be needed.

trade	adorn	precious	altar	vestments	looked	meaning

In the Middle Ages, jewels often had a religious _____, for the art of making jewellery was carefully kept up in the monasteries. Jewels were used to _____ shrines, the _____ of the priest and the vessels used in church services. These were often made of gold and decorated with _____ stones. Gradually, however, the making of jewellery became a _____ as well as an art and jewels grew to be _____ upon as part of costume.

3. Synonyms

Select the word from the list that has the most similar meaning to the word in **bold**.

Doomed	fated	intact	protected	gloomy	cheerful
Genre	attire	category	wardrobe	urban	genie
Report	conceal	hide	suppress	market	announce
Binary	double	lone	singular	purchase	advantage
Duplicate	clone	cover	send	reward	clown

4. Missing words

Choose the best word to complete the sentences.

Zinc is a soft bluish-white (1) _____ (metallic, metal, wood) which is somewhat less heavy (2) _____ (those, than, that) steel. It melts at 419 degrees Centigrade, which is well below the (3) _____ (heat, temperature, hot) of red-hot iron. Even when heated to 200 degrees Centigrade it becomes so (4) _____ (crispy, soft, brittle) that it can quite easily be crushed to powder. Zinc can be (5) _____ (squashed, roller, rolled) out into a thin sheet and in damp air becomes covered with a very thin film of tarnish.

Test 2

1. Fill in the missing words

Choose the most appropriate word from the list available to complete the following passage. One of the words will not be needed.

| attended | goddess | Earth | name | flying | protectress | husband |

Juno was the _____ the Romans gave to the queen of the gods and goddesses, whose _____ was the supreme god Jupiter. Iris, _____ of the rainbow, was Juno's messenger and she was _____ by the peacock who was said to have 100 eyes in his tail. She was queen of _____ as well as heaven and was the especial _____ of women who called upon her for help in their troubles.

2. Synonyms

Select the word from the list that has the most similar meaning to the word in **bold**.

Deplore	approve	abhor	commend	reduce	refrain
Detest	loathe	admire	cherish	approve	liken
Startle	expect	soothe	comfort	stun	finish
Conceited	diffident	arrogant	humble	weak	thin
Uproar	confusion	calm	harmony	order	whisper

3. Idioms

Match the idiom in **bold** to its meaning.

Don't give up your day job	a. Get something exactly right
Every cloud has a silver lining	b. You're not very good at this
It's a piece of cake	c. It's easy
Once in a blue moon	d. Good things come after bad things
Hit the nail on the head	e. Rarely

4. Antonyms

Select the word from the list that has the most opposite meaning to the word in **bold**.

Awake	alive	dreaming	shake	dormant	moving
Clean	soiled	rub	wipe	hoover	immaculate
Noteworthy	pad	written	important	pedestrian	notable
Secrete	reveal	discharge	perspire	hidden	undercover
Veto	ban	describe	detain	approve	bar

Test 3

1. Antonyms

Select the word from the list that has the most opposite meaning to the word in **bold**.

Narrator	speaker	listener	older	younger	storyteller
Kind	type	species	sort	class	cruel
Peripheral	edge	central	fringe	vision	sight
Jolly	awkward	miserable	nasty	upbeat	dark
Vain	narcissistic	egocentric	conceited	uncaring	modest

2. Fill in the missing words

Choose the most appropriate word from the list available to complete the following passage. One of the words will not be needed.

| brought | reign | succeeded | death | rowdy | birth | successful |

George III, who _____ his grandfather in 1760, was 22 when he began his long reign. He had been _____ up as an Englishman and was greatly interested in Britain and its empire. However his policy was not always _____ and he was largely responsible for the loss of the American colonies. Later in his _____ he suffered from fits of madness and his eldest son ruled for him, with the title of Prince Regent. When the Prince Regent became George IV, on his father's _____ in 1820, he was already 58 and had fallen into an extravagant and _____ way of life.

3. Homophones and Homographs

Homographs are two words that are spelt the same but have different meanings.
Homophones are two words that sound the same but have different meanings and spellings.

From the list below, fill in the blanks. The first one has been done for you.

| bass | bat | bow | break | brake |

1. The first time he went fishing he managed to catch a <u>bass.</u>
2. You need a _____ to play cricket.
3. Their weapons were the _____ and arrow and stones.
4. Would you like a _____ from all that hard work you've been doing?
5. Try to _____ gently when you're driving if the roads are wet.
6. Joan cannot play the _____ guitar.
7. It was dark outside when Mary noticed the _____ flying around.
8. The child was thrilled he could tie a knot and a _____.

Test 4

1. Antonyms

Select the word from the list that has the most opposite meaning to the word in **bold**.

Murmur	whisper	rumble	shout	mutter	vibration
Alarm	apprehension	dread	tension	fright	assure
Contradict	belie	repudiate	affirm	rally	deny
Boost	undermine	encourage	assist	support	spring
Perfect	improve	complete	total	corrupt	real

2. Fill in the missing words

Choose the most appropriate word from the list available to complete the following passage. One of the words will not be needed.

| sunlight | frighten | deeper | snout | streak | stripe | named |

Lantern fish generally live in the _____ parts of the oceans. There the water is cold and dark, for _____ cannot reach far below the surface. Lantern fish are so _____ because they have luminous spots on their bodies which give out light. It is likely that a sudden flash of these lights is used to _____ or dazzle a pursuer. Some lantern fish have shining dots scattered over the lower parts of their bodies and others have a large spot or _____ that gives off light above and below the base of the tail, while at least one has a large spot at the end of the _____, like the headlight of a car.

3. Idioms

Match the idiom in **bold** to its meaning.

Ignorance is bliss		a. Events have momentum and can build up
Go on a wild goose chase		b. You're better off not knowing
A snowball effect		c. Destroy relationships
Burn bridges		d. Perfect
As right as rain		e. To do something pointless

Test 5

1. Antonyms

Select the word from the list that has the most opposite meaning to the word in **bold**.

Compliant	legal	docile	yielding	meek	inflexible
Hearty	warm	weak	filling	hot	profuse
Moving	impelling	compelling	gripping	sound	stationary
Dissuade	council	encourage	thwart	remonstrate	retire
End	culminate	terminate	commence	conclude	expire

2. Fill in the missing words

Choose the most appropriate word from the list available to complete the following passage. One of the words will not be needed.

damage	grey	distinctive	humid	confused	base	mould

Camellia flower blight can be easily _____ with frost damage or grey mould. Frost _____ is normally confined to the edges of the petals or, in severe cases, affects the whole flower at once. Grey _____ can cause similar brown flecks, but will also produce fuzzy, grey growth under _____ conditions. Camellia flower blight has the _____, diagnostic feature of a ring of white fungal growth visible around the _____ of the petals.

3. Synonyms

Select the word from the list that has the most similar meaning to the word in **bold**.

Brag	conceal	crow	hide	sack	hole
Brawl	agree	soup	tussle	bowl	concur
Range	array	singular	organise	type	divide
Deploy	finish	conclude	commence	create	use
Showy	ornate	inferior	modest	humble	theatrical

4. Missing words

Choose the best word to complete the sentences.

Wool is widely used for making (1) _____ (hot, tepid, warm) clothing. Most of it comes from sheep, although wool from other (2) _____ (rodents, animals, goats) is used as well. These include the Angora rabbit, the Angora goat, the camel, the Kashmir goat, the Peruvian goat, the llama and the (3) _____ (rhino, alpaca, armadillo). Some of these animals (4) _____ (grew, grown, grow) two different types of wool, or hair, which is a better name for it. Some camels have an inner coat of short, soft hair that can be made into coats and a shaggy outer coat of long (5) _____ (course, corse, coarse) hair that is spun and woven into heavy driving belts for machinery.

Test 6

1. Fill in the missing words

Choose the most appropriate word from the list available to complete the following passage. One of the words will not be needed.

| lies | country | trade | ridge | important | island | farther |

Jamaica is one of the most _____ islands in the Caribbean Sea and is an independent _____ of the Commonwealth of Nations. It is roughly the same size as Northern Ireland and _____ about 100 miles south of Cuba. Somewhat _____ distant to the east across the Jamaica Channel is the island of Hispaniola, now divided into two countries, Haiti and the Dominican Republic. Jamaica is a very mountainous _____. A _____ of high land runs along the island, rising in the east to the Blue Mountains with a peak of 7402ft, the highest in the West Indies.

2. Synonyms

Select the word from the list that has the most similar meaning to the word in **bold**.

Counsel	parliament	government	discourage	advise	mislead
Mock	deride	compliment	flatter	fan	travel
Artificial	plain	bogus	simple	genuine	natural
Burrow	cover	delve	lend	fill	return
Clog	block	assistance	run	promotion	work

3. Idioms

Match the idiom in **bold** to its meaning.

Once bitten, twice shy	a. We agree
On cloud nine	b. You're more cautious a second time
We see eye to eye	c. Everything is going wrong at once
Through thick and thin	d. Very happy
When it rains it pours	e. In good times and in bad times

4. Antonyms

Select the word from the list that has the most opposite meaning to the word in **bold**.

Sanction	accredit	certify	oppose	credit	loan
Arduous	facile	onerous	laborious	gruelling	work
Total	addition	part	divide	complete	instant
Useless	futile	idle	valuable	expensive	costly
Vacant	married	single	engaged	asleep	homeless

Test 7

1. Antonyms

Select the word from the list that has the most opposite meaning to the word in **bold**.

Remiss	culpable	slack	careful	sloppy	pass
Sell	purchase	vend	exchange	return	trade
Sane	lucid	stable	right	irrational	sound
Grip	restraint	constraint	release	realise	return
Credible	believable	tenable	doubtful	possible	real

2. Fill in the missing words

Choose the most appropriate word from the list available to complete the following passage. One of the words will not be needed.

finlets	eddies	handsome	roam	water	shoals	relatives

The mackerel is a _____, streamlined fish whose second dorsal fin and the anal fin are divided into a number of small separate _____ above and below the tail. These control the flow of water over the tail as the fish swims, so that _____ do not form and slow the fish down. That is why the mackerel and its _____, the bonitos and tunnies, are among the fastest of fish and are able to move quickly for long periods. They _____ the ocean in great _____, feeding on the small fish, crustacea and other creatures near the surface.

3. Synonyms

Select the word from the list that has the most similar meaning to the word in **bold**.

Pragmatic	idealistic	stupid	theoretical	efficient	wavy
Clothe	drape	disrobe	open	wardrobe	unravel
Vista	credit	payment	creation	period	landscape
Token	measure	symbol	length	ride	over
Depression	rise	success	deflation	calm	modesty

Test 8

1. Antonyms

Select the word from the list that has the most opposite meaning to the word in **bold**.

Persuade	coax	entice	exhort	incline	deter
Boom	reverberate	resound	recession	trail	explode
Havoc	calm	mayhem	desolation	wreckage	calamity
Factual	precise	fictitious	unbiased	valid	literal
Contradict	contravene	counter	fight	traverse	endorse

2. Fill in the missing words

Choose the most appropriate word from the list available to complete the following passage. One of the words will not be needed.

related	adder	species	coiled	commonly	slender	poison

Mamba is the name given to a group of _____, active snakes some of which live in trees. They are closely _____ to the cobras and are often called tree-cobras. Because of the strength of their _____, mambas are among the most dangerous of poisonous snakes. They are found in tropical and southern Africa. There are several _____ of mambas. Some are bright leaf-green in colour which makes them very difficult to see when they are _____ among the leaves of a tree. These are called green mambas. Others are a dark, gun-metal grey and are _____ known as black mambas.

3. Odd one out

Four of the words in the list are linked in some way. Mark the word that is not linked, as shown in the example.

Example:	dove	crow	~~cat~~	magpie	eagle
1.	division	equation	subtraction	addition	multiplication
2.	house	flat	car	bungalow	mansion
3.	eyes	nose	legs	mouth	ears
4.	north	below	south	west	east
5.	five	seven	eleven	half	twelve

Test 9

1. Fill in the missing words

Choose the most appropriate word from the list available to complete the following passage. One of the words will not be needed.

| native | clusters | sycamore | cattle | spice | sugar | winged |

The maple family includes the _____. Like the sycamore, the field maple has _____ seeds which are carried by the wind. The field maple is _____ to Great Britain. Maple leaves, which contain _____, are glossy and are divided round their edges into five parts. They used to be collected as food for _____, as cows enjoyed them. The yellow-green flowers, which open in May and June, stand up in little _____.

2. Synonyms

Select the word from the list that has the most similar meaning to the word in **bold**.

Shop	sell	produce	manufacture	boutique	purchase
Avoid	face	dodge	meet	allow	seek
Authenticate	deny	disapprove	invalidate	substantiate	real
Abundance	need	poverty	scarcity	profusion	simple
Clemency	cruelty	satsuma	mercy	orange	meanness

3. Idioms

Match the idiom in **bold** to its meaning.

A blessing in disguise	a. Better to arrive late than not at all
Better late than never	b. Unwell
So far so good	c. I have no idea
Your guess is as good as mine	d. Things are going well so far
Under the weather	e. A good thing that seemed bad at first

4. Antonyms

Select the word from the list that has the most opposite meaning to the word in **bold**.

Circumvent	avoid	deceive	crimp	confront	circumference
Civilized	quiet	primitive	educated	polite	tolerant
Chronological	late	after	before	random	ordered
Compliance	agreement	assent	descent	resistance	submission
Dominant	ruling	superior	inconspicuous	major	paramount

Test 10

1. Antonyms

Select the word from the list that has the most opposite meaning to the word in **bold**.

Extrovert	showstopper	exhibitionist	introvert	chic	minuscule
Minimum	grain	margin	maximum	iota	large
Fidelity	allegiance	ardour	constancy	enmity	loyalty
Harmony	consensus	discord	consistency	peace	kinship
Valuable	asset	commodity	worthless	expensive	benefit

2. Fill in the missing words

Choose the most appropriate word from the list available to complete the following passage. One of the words will not be needed.

rapidly	connected	buses	shaft	economical	gearing	cylinders

Diesel engines, which work in the same way as those of motor _____ and lorries, came _____ into use for driving ships after World War I. Those used in big ships are generally large, heavy engines with anything up to eight _____. Smaller ships may use high-speed diesels _____ to the propeller shafts either by mechanical _____ or, in diesel-electric ships, by using alternators and electric motors like those for turbo-electric drive. Diesel engines are _____, giving more power for each ton of fuel burnt than any other kind.

3. Odd one out

Four of the words in the list are linked in some way. Mark the word that is not linked, as shown in the example.

Example:	dove	crow	~~cat~~	magpie	eagle
1.	piano	stool	flute	trumpet	clarinet
2.	love	hatred	fear	greed	anger
3.	dog	cat	monkey	dragon	horse
4.	mother	friend	daughter	son	father
5.	shoe	sandal	boot	glove	trainer

Test 11

1. Antonyms

Select the word from the list that has the most opposite meaning to the word in **bold**.

Popular	trendy	prominent	beloved	keen	obscure
Resolute	adamant	complacent	staunch	serious	stubborn
Zany	comical	slow	eccentric	wild	serious
Unkempt	neglected	scruffy	bedraggled	ordered	chaotic
Permanent	ephemeral	durable	fast	lasting	barn

2. Fill in the missing words

Choose the most appropriate word from the list available to complete the following passage. One of the words will not be needed.

| mechanism | pollinated | reproductive | evolved | permit | tree | fertilise |

The flower is the _____ structure of flowering plants, which gives rise to seeds and fruit. The flower provides a _____ for pollen from the male part of the flower to _____ the egg cells in the female part of the flower. The flowers may develop or be constructed in such a way as to encourage cross-pollination between different flowers, or _____ self-pollination within the same flower. Many plants have _____ to produce large, colourful flowers that are attractive to animal pollinators, others have evolved to produce dull, scentless flowers that are _____ by the wind.

3. Homophones and Homographs

Homographs are two words that are spelt the same but have different meanings.
Homophones are two words that sound the same but have different meanings and spellings.

From the list below, fill in the blanks. The first one has been done for you.

| flour | entrance | flower | moped | row |

1. After making bread she had ____flour____ all over her apron.
2. She asked him to _____ across the lake as she felt tired.
3. He could not afford a motorbike so bought a cheaper _____ instead.
4. The groom wore a beautiful _____ in his lapel on his wedding day.
5. She was very miserable and _____ around the house all day.
6. She did not want to _____ with him so agreed with his suggestion.
7. The book describes his _____ into politics.
8. The thief gained _____ via the backdoor.

Test 12

1. Synonyms

Select the word from the list that has the most similar meaning to the word in **bold**.

Family	outside	clan	familiar	home	friend
Altitude	elevation	depth	below	temperature	barometer
Vain	humble	modest	arrogant	artery	heart
Antagonist	ally	enemy	assistant	uncle	relative
Fake	honesty	original	friend	foe	hoax

2. Fill in the missing words

Choose the most appropriate word from the list available to complete the following passage. One of the words will not be needed.

formation	categorised	biscuit	rind	bland	improves	ripen

Cheese is distinguished by its flavour: _____, like Edam, or powerfully strong, like Provolone. It is also _____ according to texture: fresh, soft, semi-hard or hard. Cheese may be identified partly by the _____ of the rind. The rind protects the cheese's interior and allows it to _____ properly. Apart from those with a manufactured wax coating, such as Edam or Gouda, there are those with a dry or natural _____, such as Stilton. Some cheeses are bathed in a brine solution. This hardens the rind and _____ the flavour of the body.

3. Idioms

Match the idiom in **bold** to its meaning.

The best of both worlds	a. Doing a good job
Hang in there	b. Where either of two choices are advantageous
On the ball	c. To joke with someone
Pull someone's leg	d. It's raining heavily
It's raining cats and dogs	e. Don't give up

Test 13

1. Antonyms

Select the word from the list that has the most opposite meaning to the word in **bold**.

Beleaguer	annoy	beset	plague	assist	diseased
Logical	cogent	legitimate	lucid	plausible	irrational
Destitute	affluent	homeless	exhausted	empty	insolvent
Idle	fast	stationary	lazy	slow	active
Absurd	ludicrous	sane	foolish	quick	senseless

2. Fill in the missing words

Choose the most appropriate word from the list available to complete the following passage. One of the words will not be needed.

protein	carnivorous	plentiful	ethical	beef	outweigh	energies

From the earliest times, man has been a _____ animal. Because meat provides so much _____ and essential vitamins, early people could spend less of their time eating and could successfully turn their _____ to activities which in time placed them above their peers. Meat was, from the beginning, equated with life and early hunting was designed to supply a _____ amount of animals. Though today there is a reappraisal of the importance of meat in the diet - whether its drawbacks like cholesterol and high price _____ its value as a protein provider, or, in the case of vegetarians, an _____ consideration - meat is still one of the most expensive items on the shopping list.

3. Odd one out

Four of the words in the list are linked in some way. Mark the word that is not linked, as shown in the example.

Example:	dove	crow	~~cat~~	magpie	eagle
1.	lake	forest	ocean	river	sea
2.	happy	elated	cheerful	grumpy	joyous
3.	beef	pork	chicken	peas	lamb
4.	apple	banana	asparagus	peach	plum
5.	silver	gold	tin	paper	lead

Test 14

1. Antonyms

Select the word from the list that has the most opposite meaning to the word in **bold**.

Release	clemency	discharge	commute	breathe	restraint
Evict	dislodge	oust	vote	expel	admit
Evoke	arouse	elicit	repress	conjure	provoke
Linger	dawdle	drift	stay	advance	hesitate
Commence	start	stop	run	walk	drift

2. Fill in the missing words

Choose the most appropriate word from the list available to complete the following passage. One of the words will not be needed.

amongst	repute	teacher	thought	urban	emphasis	directed

The educational _____ of our time has been chiefly _____ toward the improvement of city school systems. So we hear of the great schools in London, Manchester, Birmingham and Edinburgh _____ other places; but we have yet to hear of a single county or village of rural population, the excellence of whose schools entitles them to national _____. The emphasis of our thought has been placed long and hard on _____ schools at the expense of the rural schools. It is time to change the _____ of our ideas and to consider the necessities of the rural schools.

3. Synonyms

Select the word from the list that has the most similar meaning to the word in **bold**.

Inane	blend	daft	mix	considered	more
Merciful	cruel	harsh	mean	lenient	tight
Considerate	generous	mean	obtuse	hateful	careless
Frank	abnormal	blunt	dishonest	ambiguous	kind
Legitimate	lawful	mean	criminal	dishonest	illogical

Test 15

1. Antonyms

Select the word from the list that has the most opposite meaning to the word in **bold**.

Barbaric	brutal	cruel	coarse	primitive	cultured
Wholly	religious	totally	untrue	partially	undone
Obtuse	dense	intelligent	insensitive	opaque	calm
Plunge	spree	dive	fall	rise	swim
Decelerate	slow	accent	ascent	accelerate	walk

2. Fill in the missing words

Choose the most appropriate word from the list available to complete the following passage. One of the words will not be needed.

| evergreen | joints | pruning | tactfully | option | badly | estimated |

The range of conifers available is so wide that there is an _____ for almost every space. You can choose from _____ or deciduous conifers; blue, green or yellow foliage; and a wide range of growth habits. The speed at which a conifer will grow can often be _____ by looking at the size of the previous season's extension growth; otherwise look at the plant's growth habit with a view to _____ or shaping. For example, a pine or Abies has obvious branch _____ where pruning cuts can be made _____ and without spoiling the look of the plant. By contrast, something more globular and rounded in shape, such as Cryptomeria, is usually best if just left to grow.

31

3. Synonyms

Select the word from the list that has the most similar meaning to the word in **bold**.

Gregarious	cold	affable	unfriendly	loud	meagre
Compassion	empathy	warm	animosity	hatred	tyranny
Coy	aggressive	bashful	backward	impudent	poor
Fatal	long	frighten	mortal	short	cruel
Override	allow	enforce	approve	shout	annul

Test 16

1. Fill in the missing words

Choose the most appropriate word from the list available to complete the following passage. One of the words will not be needed.

| pauper | aristocrat | properties | products | delicate | translucency | compound |

Porcelain is the _____ of clay bodies, the most highly refined of all clay body types. It is rarely found as a natural body but is a _____ of a blend of kaolins, china clays, ball clays and feldspars. Porcelain's characteristic _____ include: an extreme fineness of grain structure, hardness and toughness when fired, resistance to acids and _____. Its colour is usually white or blue-white when fired. Porcelain _____ are usually thin-walled and should be handled with care as they are extremely _____.

2. Idioms

Match the idiom in **bold** to its meaning.

Give someone the cold shoulder	a. Make people feel more comfortable
On thin ice	b. Ignore someone
Break the ice	c. You're just as bad as they are
It takes one to know one	d. Fix the problem now or it will get worse later
A stitch in time saves nine	e. If you make another mistake there will be trouble

3. Homophones and Homographs

Homographs are two words that are spelt the same but have different meanings.
Homophones are two words that sound the same but have different meanings and spellings.

From the list below, fill in the blanks. The first one has been done for you.

| die | minute | dye | down | fine |

1. He knew he would ____die____ if he drank the poison.
2. She held the duckling in her hand and could feel its soft _____.
3. Oliver could only just see the small key it was so _____.
4. "Wait a _____!" he shouted, "I'm just coming."
5. If you park on a restricted road you risk being charged a _____
6. Jane would have to _____ her blouse if she wanted to change the colour.
7. He knew everything would be _____ if he arrived on time.
8. He looked _____ the well and could just see the water below.

Test 17

1. Antonyms

Select the word from the list that has the most opposite meaning to the word in **bold**.

Advanced	exceptional	behind	progressive	followed	forward
Stout	slight	burly	portly	small	bulky
Annul	abrogate	cancel	declare	enact	quash
Upset	capsize	derange	disarray	invert	order
Cajole	wheedle	dupe	entice	repulse	juggle

2. Odd one out

Four of the words in the list are linked in some way. Mark the word that is not linked, as shown in the example.

Example:	dove	crow	~~cat~~	magpie	eagle
1.	walk	jog	run	sit	shuffle
2.	tango	rumba	waltz	run	samba
3.	pencil	paper	pen	crayon	chalk
4.	milk	cheese	yogurt	bread	butter
5.	arrow	spear	dagger	shield	knife

3. Missing words

Choose the best word to complete the sentences.

The yellow and black wasps that (1) _____ (entrance, enter, entry) houses or make themselves a nuisance around food come from nests where they live with many hundreds or even thousands of sister-wasps and the (2) _____ (queen, king, cavalier). Each nest is (3) _____ (start, started, starting) by the queen wasp. She comes out of her winter sleep in the spring and (4) _____ (choice, chose, chooses) a place in which to set up home, in the ground or perhaps in a hollow tree, according to the kind of wasp she is. The nest she makes is usually grey and (5) _____ (hung, hangs, hang) down from the roof of the nesting place, attached to a little stalk.

Test 18

1. Antonyms

Select the word from the list that has the most opposite meaning to the word in **bold**.

Augment	amplify	abridge	boost	develop	expand
Trail	chase	lead	pull	dally	track
Sound	resonate	burst	bubble	blare	unstable
Strapping	sturdy	attenuated	brawny	hefty	tied
Pollute	foul	poison	clean	infect	carbon

2. Synonyms

Select the word from the list that has the most similar meaning to the word in **bold**.

Deputy	headmaster	ambassador	teacher	commission	march
Deed	inertia	failure	rest	action	exist
Cancel	sanction	build	abort	continue	ratify
Deplore	approve	mourn	endorse	laud	revel
Flamboyant	plain	quiet	simple	moderate	dazzling

3. Odd one out

Four of the words in the list are linked in some way. Mark the word that is not linked, as shown in the example.

Example: dove   crow   ~~cat~~   magpie   eagle

1. how   cow   low   now   pow
2. Earth   Mercury   Sun   Venus   Jupiter
3. September   April   June   January   November
4. March   September   July   January   December
5. jacket   trousers   shoes   cloth   hat

Test 19

1. Fill in the missing words

Choose the most appropriate word from the list available to complete the following passage. One of the words will not be needed.

| grilling | tenderest | shoulders | cattle | gentle | sirloin | yield |

As a rule of thumb, when it comes to beef, those parts of the animal at the top, along the centre back to the rump end, are the _____ and that makes them well-suited to fast cooking methods such as roasting, _____ and frying. The _____ and lower legs of the cow, the parts that are worked hardest when the animal is alive, _____ up tougher cuts which are usually cheaper and blessed with lots of flavour, but they require long and _____ cooking. When roasting beef, the larger the joint the better. Forerib is the best of all, but _____ comes a close second.

2. Idioms

Match the idiom in **bold** to its meaning.

An apple a day keeps the doctor away	a. Everything, the whole way
Bolt from the blue	b. Eating nutritious food is good for you
Calm before the storm	c. The issue that people are avoiding
The whole nine yards	d. Something that happened without warning
The elephant in the room	e. It's fine now but something bad is coming

3. Synonyms

Select the word from the list that has the most similar meaning to the word in **bold**.

Wharf	short	dock	guzzle	frenzy	beach
Thwart	impede	facilitate	aid	assist	borrow
Bogus	authentic	factual	spurious	common	rare
Graft	rest	work	separate	divide	ongoing
Eloquence	inability	weak	dull	fluency	tending

Test 20

1. Antonyms

Select the word from the list that has the most opposite meaning to the word in **bold**.

Harmless	safe	poisonous	dangerous	careful	slow
Prodigal	last	profligate	wanton	needy	careful
Swift	speedy	moving	crafty	slow	fast
Lean	skinny	tall	wide	fatty	muscular
Rural	farmland	city	town	urban	inside

2. Synonyms

Select the word from the list that has the most similar meaning to the word in **bold**.

Revere	abhor	admire	condemn	polish	despise
Gauge	assess	ruler	height	level	port
Impair	diminish	develop	enlarge	aid	expand
Judicious	ignorant	jury	judge	astute	demand
Rhetoric	quiet	mean	oratory	cruel	harsh

3. Missing words

Choose the best word to complete the sentences.

Subtraction is a (1) _____ (procedure, process, product) in simple arithmetic which is closely connected to addition. The putting (2) _____ (together, apart, onto) of numbers to make a larger number is addition, but subtraction is the taking away of a number from a larger number to see how many are left. For example, 5 add 3 (3) _____ (equates, equator, equals) 8, but 5 subtract 3 equals 2. In a subtraction sum the answer is called the (4) _____ (reminder, remainder, remorse) or the difference. Subtraction is represented by a short (5) _____ (dish, dash, dot) mark.

Test 21

1. Antonyms

Select the word from the list that has the most opposite meaning to the word in **bold**.

Concise	pithy	succinct	wordy	brief	dictionary
Taut	tight	tightrope	looped	loose	long
Encumber	facilitate	burden	disengage	tighten	lengthen
Separate	unite	detach	terrace	divide	cleave
Climb	clamber	mount	scale	descent	linger

2. Fill in the missing words

Choose the most appropriate word from the list available to complete the following passage. One of the words will not be needed.

hedgerows	spiny	bitter	seldom	shrub	ancestor	borne

The wild crab apple is the _____ of all apples. It is a native tree of Britain and is common in woods and _____ everywhere except the north of Scotland. It _____ grows to a greater height than thirty feet. The shape of the crab apple varies a great deal, but the branches are usually spreading and slightly drooping and the twigs are _____. The rose-pink, sometimes pinkish-white flowers appear just before the leaves in April and look lovely as they are _____ in clusters on short shoots. The apples ripen in October. They are small and may be either yellow or red. Whichever colour they are they are much too _____ to eat, but can be made into excellent jelly.

3. Odd one out

Four of the words in the list are linked in some way. Mark the word that is not linked, as shown in the example.

Example: dove   crow   ~~cat~~   magpie   eagle

1. banana   apple   almond   plum   orange
2. listen   swim   walk   run   climb
3. drill   hammer   screwdriver   wood   pliers
4. ant   fly   beetle   dog   wasp
5. bake   peel   fry   roast   grill

Test 22

1. Fill in the missing words

Choose the most appropriate word from the list available to complete the following passage. One of the words will not be needed.

| determined | remarried | magistrate | carving | block | foster | profession |

Michelangelo was born in Italy in 1475. His father was a _____ and proud of his noble ancestry. The family moved to Florence shortly after Michelangelo was born and he was placed in the care of a _____ mother who lived just outside the city. Michelangelo's mother died when he was six years old and his father _____. From a young age he was _____ to be a sculptor but his father thought this was not a worthy _____ for the son of a noble house. Despite this he went on to become one of the world's greatest artists. In 1501 he sculpted the famous statue of David from a _____ of marble that had been lying in a courtyard for a hundred years.

2. Synonyms

Select the word from the list that has the most similar meaning to the word in **bold**.

Emit	hide	conceal	take	emanate	donate
Eddy	vortex	space	moon	galaxy	planet
Assumption	fact	hunch	knowledge	intelligence	proof
Omit	keep	note	heed	attend	neglect
Cove	brush	bay	pier	beach	headland

3. Idioms

Match the idiom in **bold** to its meaning.

A storm in a teacup		a. That's true, I agree
To get bent out of shape		b. A big fuss about a small problem
You can say that again		c. To get upset
Go back to the drawing board		d. To not hold someone responsible for something
Let someone off the hook		e. Start all over again

Test 23

1. Fill in the missing words

Choose the most appropriate word from the list available to complete the following passage. One of the words will not be needed.

| fuse | seconds | tossed | roar | crust | shore | bottomless |

I picked up the fuse and opened my lantern to get a light. Then I lit the _____ and made sure it was burning well. I raced back to the raft. Hans pushed off. At a safe distance from _____ we waited. The _____ ticked by. Suddenly, the rock exploded. We stared into a _____ pit. The sea swelled into a great wave and the raft _____ madly. We were thrown to the deck and there was no light. In the darkness the _____ of water filled my ears. We had blown up a rock which blocked the entrance to a pit leading down to the centre of the Earth.

2. Synonyms

Select the word from the list that has the most similar meaning to the word in **bold**.

Snippet	divide	cut	whole	divide	fragment
Designate	decide	nominate	concur	mark	note
Marginal	minor	important	edge	central	ruled
Quaint	normal	grave	small	enormous	peculiar
Sect	fraction	faction	fiction	factual	creation

3. Idioms

Match the idiom in **bold** to its meaning.

It's not rocket science		a. It's too late
Miss the boat		b. My patience has run out
No pain no gain		c. To reveal a secret
That's the last straw		d. It's not complicated
Let the cat out of the bag		e. You have to work hard to get what you want

Test 24

1. Antonyms

Select the word from the list that has the most opposite meaning to the word in **bold**.

Beautify	mar	decorate	guild	dress	clamour
Eschew	renounce	shun	leave	deport	keep
Luminous	lucid	dull	lustrous	vivid	damp
Gloomy	dreary	sharpen	sombre	hopeful	dismal
Dampen	dehydrate	moisten	sprinkle	sparkle	reduce

2. Homophones and Homographs

Homographs are two words that are spelt the same but have different meanings.
Homophones are two words that sound the same but have different meanings and spellings.

From the list below, fill in the blanks. The first one has been done for you.

| wound | contract | wave | hour | our |

1. After taking a tumble, Emma realised the ___wound___ on her leg was quite bad.

2. Jack _____ the crown on his watch to change the time.

3. Carol read the _____ before signing it.

4. But he had to _____ his hand high if she was to notice him.

5. The surfer suddenly stood up and balanced on his board on the high _____.

6. "It was _____ fault" I said, "we didn't see him coming".

7. She was due to arrive on the _____ but was running late.

8. Peter was worried he may _____ the disease if he wasn't immunised.

3. Odd one out

Four of the words in the list are linked in some way. Mark the word that is not linked, as shown in the example.

Example: dove   crow   ~~cat~~   magpie   eagle

1. London   Dublin   Canberra   Newcastle   Paris
2. helium   oxygen   hydrogen   aluminium   nitrogen
3. stool   table   chair   bench   sofa
4. England   France   Africa   Poland   Sweden
5. guitar   viola   clarinet   violin   cello

Test 25

1. Antonyms

Select the word from the list that has the most opposite meaning to the word in **bold**.

Permanent	long	tighten	temporary	durable	perpetual
Calibrate	average	check	compute	balance	destroy
Strife	bickering	clash	discord	agreement	work
Permit	allow	prevent	below	licence	agree
Restrict	flow	move	curb	develop	wider

2. Synonyms

Select the word from the list that has the most similar meaning to the word in **bold**.

Lurch	steady	careen	tall	stride	delve
Carp	approve	compliment	talk	shout	quibble
Sporadic	common	even	irregular	singular	foliage
Prune	clip	divide	vegetable	health	dine
Ancillary	chief	additional	soldier	medicine	post

3. Missing words

Choose the best word to complete the sentences.

Teeth are used to chew food before (1) _____ (swallows, swallowed, swallowing) it. Human teeth also help in speech, for they help to (2) _____ (form, force, ford) certain sounds. Each tooth is divided into two main parts. In the gum is a root (3) _____ (anchoring, taking, forcing) the tooth to the jawbone and the part that can be seen in the mouth is called the crown. The part of the tooth (4) _____ (were, where, with) the crown and root meet is called the neck. The crown is covered with a very hard (5) _____ (produce, substance, mercantile) called enamel. The main bulk of the tooth is made of dentine, which resembles ivory.

Test 26

1. Fill in the missing words

Choose the most appropriate word from the list available to complete the following passage. One of the words will not be needed.

| naturally | cities | surface | spores | maintain | springs | ejects |

There are many types of ponds to explore, even in busy towns and _____.

Wherever water collects for any length of time, new life _____ rapidly into being.

You can test this fact for yourself by sinking a bowl into the ground and letting it fill _____ with rainwater. Before many days have passed, you will see that a green scum is beginning to cover the _____. This is called algae and it has grown from _____ so tiny you cannot see them with the naked eye, you need a microscope.

Algae gives off oxygen. All animals need oxygen to live so although this green scum may not look very attractive it is essential to _____ life in the water.

2. Odd one out

Four of the words in the list are linked in some way. Mark the word that is not linked, as shown in the example.

Example: dove   crow   ~~cat~~   magpie   eagle

1. scarf   tie   necklace   collar   sock
2. pongy   whiffy   smelly   tasty   malodorous
3. did   had   were   will   went
4. clown   ringmaster doctor   juggler   acrobat
5. stalls   balcony   auditorium stage   school

3. Antonyms

Select the word from the list that has the most opposite meaning to the word in **bold**.

Flagrant	glaring	smelly	odorous	delicate	under
Insidious	subtle	astute	perilous	sincere	artful
Laconic	pithy	terse	crisp	slow	verbose
Vilify	assail	flatter	smear	decry	revile
Puerile	mature	clean	pure	tainted	foolish

Test 27

1. Antonyms

Select the word from the list that has the most opposite meaning to the word in **bold**.

Strange	bizarre	aberrant	normal	rare	clear
Encourage	advocate	block	bolster	spur	stun
Enlarge	broaden	magnify	swell	reduce	create
Liberate	detach	detain	redeem	save	late
Impartial	candid	equitable	dislike	disown	prejudiced

2. Synonyms

Select the word from the list that has the most similar meaning to the word in **bold**.

Yearn	abjure	dislike	sew	cotton	covet
Gradient	mark	judge	incline	score	total
Avid	ardent	cool	hot	digest	ingest
Dormant	alert	inert	active	run	open
Trench	border	edge	centre	outside	gully

3. Missing letters

Fill in the missing letters to complete the words.

Beside the Thames, on the east side of the City of London, stands the __/n/ /i/e/ /t__ Tower of London. It has been a palace, a __/o/r/t/ /e/s/__, a mint and a prison. Many famous people, queens, dukes and churchmen, have been __e/x/e/ /u/ /e/__, murdered or imprisoned there. It is perhaps the most __h/i/ /t/o/ / /c__ building in England. Today the Tower is an ancient __m/o/ /u/ /e/n/__ but it is also used as a barracks and the crown jewels are kept there. The Tower is __g/u/ /r/ /e/__ by the Yeoman Warders.

Test 28

1. Antonyms

Select the word from the list that has the most opposite meaning to the word in **bold**.

Break	cleft	fracture	breach	juncture	lunch
Familiar	mundane	intimate	domestic	relative	alien
Biased	partisan	impartial	led	followed	meek
Allay	calm	incite	ease	lessen	mitigate
Just	corrupt	ethical	decent	aloof	normal

2. Idioms

Match the idiom in **bold** to its meaning.

Good things come to those who wait	a. Just barely
By the skin of your teeth	b. To make a mistake but to learn from it
Comparing apples to oranges	c. It's your decision
Live and learn	d. Be patient
The ball is in your court	e. Comparing two things that cannot be compared

3. Missing letters

Fill in the missing letters to complete the words.

Porridge is a popular **b/r/ / /k/f/ /s/t** food on cold days. It is usually made using milk, but can also be made using **w/ /t/ /r**. Some people like to **/w/e/ /t/ /n** it with sugar or dried fruit. It is a good idea to stir your porridge as you make it to avoid it **b/ /c/o/ /i/ /g** lumpy. Scottish people like to sprinkle salt onto their porridge. Historically porridge was served in **/p/e/c/ /a/** bowls called porringers.

Test 29

1. Idioms

Match the idiom in **bold** to its meaning.

Bite the bullet	a. Tell something briefly
Get your act together	b. Go to sleep
Hit the sack	c. To get something that is inevitable done
Make a long story short	d. Slow down
Easy does it	e. Work better

2. Odd one out

Four of the words in the list are linked in some way. Mark the word that is not linked, as shown in the example:

Example :   dove   crow   ~~cat~~   magpie   eagle

1. Mrs   Miss   Master   Madam   Ms
2. doctor   nurse   consultant   solicitor   surgeon
3. crow   eagle   emu   albatross   robin
4. depart   exit   withdraw   arrive   vacate
5. terrier   poodle   siamese   greyhound   collie

3. Antonyms

Select the word from the list that has the most opposite meaning to the word in **bold**.

Noxious	sterile	fetid	baneful	absurd	outrageous
Plethora	deluge	surfeit	flood	scarcity	total
Probity	corruption	rectitude	integrity	fidelity	criminal
Sanguine	cheerful	buoyant	enthusiastic	pessimistic	sober
Stolid	bovine	dense	inert	lively	gaseous

Test 30

1. Fill in the missing words

Choose the most appropriate word from the list available to complete the following passage. One of the words will not be needed.

| massive | ammonia | largest | surrounded | moon | ancient | raged |

Jupiter is the fifth planet from our Sun and is, by far, the _____ planet in the solar system. It is more than twice as _____ as all the other planets combined. Jupiter's stripes and swirls are actually cold, windy clouds of _____ and water, floating in an atmosphere of hydrogen and helium. Jupiter's iconic Great Red Spot is a giant storm bigger than Earth that has _____ for hundreds of years. Jupiter is _____ by 79 known moons. Scientists are most interested in the four largest moons discovered by Galileo Galilei in 1610: Io, Europa, Ganymede and Callisto. Jupiter is named for the king of the _____ Roman gods.

2. Synonyms

Select the word from the list that has the most similar meaning to the word in **bold**.

Evaluate	neglect	appraise	sum	financial	govern
Clause	passage	total	feet	hands	whole
Rampant	fragrant	flagrant	flagging	beat	time
Sly	foolish	inept	high	mean	astute
Hospitable	cold	heartless	friendly	dark	ambulance

3. Antonyms

Select the word from the list that has the most opposite meaning to the word in **bold**.

Swarthy	light	strong	weak	dagger	shield
Torpid	heavy	dull	languid	active	fast
Rife	rampant	replete	limited	knife	fork
Quixotic	cautious	foolish	dreamy	utopian	organised
Hapless	woeful	wretched	slow	straight	fortuitous

Test 31

1. Fill in the missing words

Choose the most appropriate word from the list available to complete the following passage. Two of the words will not be needed.

| massive | urban | declined | rural | form | deny | climate |

Over recent years, many of our once-common butterflies have _____ dramatically in number due to increased development, agricultural intensification, habitat loss and _____ change; for instance, the small tortoiseshell has decreased by a _____ 80% in South East England since 1990. But butterflies do have a lifeline. Together, the 16 million gardens across the UK _____ an area for wildlife larger than all our National Nature Reserves. This patchwork of habitats helps our wildlife to move about freely, forming a vast living landscape that links _____ green spaces with the wider countryside.

2. Synonyms

Select the word from the list that has the most similar meaning to the word in **bold**.

Gorge	abstain	fast	slow	devour	mountain
Flout	approve	commend	bake	wear	mock
Toll	dwarf	levy	bridge	work	pension
Truce	amnesty	continuation	war	persistance	forego
Eerie	cellar	creepy	earthly	common	rare

3. Homophones and Homographs

Homographs are two words that are spelt the same but have different meanings.
Homophones are two words that sound the same but have different meanings and spellings.

From the list below, fill in the blanks. The first one has been done for you.

| axes | content | band | knight | night |

1. Jake took two ____axes____ with him to chop down the tree.

2. "What time of _____ do you call this young lady?" her father asked.

3. She always tied her hair in a _____.

4. Six planets in our solar system rotate in the same direction on their _____.

5. She was _____ with the standard of her work.

6. Marion had never seen a _____ before and was very impressed.

7. The _____ of the book disappointed Tom and he could not finish it.

8. Chris desperately wanted to sing in a _____ but he was tone deaf.

Test 32

1. Antonyms

Select the word from the list that has the most opposite meaning to the word in bold.

Hard	vulnerable	solid	strong	tough	callous
Amass	donate	divide	large	small	gather
Composure	agitation	aplomb	dignity	create	accord
Complacent	free	troubled	calm	serene	miserable
Hoard	stash	scatter	group	acquire	cache

2. Odd one out

Four of the words in the list are linked in some way. Mark the word that is not linked, as shown in the example.

Example: dove   crow   ~~cat~~   magpie   eagle

1. wink   stare   pout   blink   see
2. ankle   wrist   elbow   knee   bicep
3. femur   ulna   radius   scapula   deltoid
4. meadow   pasture   mountain   lea   field
5. gram   kilogram ounce   metre   ton

3. Missing letters

Fill in the missing letters to complete the words.

The raven **b/ / /o/ /g/s** to the crow family. It is a large, entirely black bird, very like the carrion crow in **a/ /p/ /a/r/ /n/c/e** but bigger. It croaks, but can utter other sounds as well and is able to **/i/m/ /c** other birds. Ravens live mostly in **/o/u/ /t/ /i/n** areas in Great Britain and by the sea. Their nests are built in cliffs and **q/u/ /r/ /i/ /s** or sometimes in trees and are made of sticks and stems mixed with earth and lined with moss, hair and wool.

Test 33

1. Antonyms

Select the word from the list that has the most opposite meaning to the word in **bold**.

Deteriorate	improve	degrade	ebb	fade	chaos
Apathetic	passive	stoic	cold	caring	strong
Local	resident	native	alien	traveller	close
Dismantle	raze	repair	annihilate	destroy	take
Overlook	sign	miss	notice	view	screen

2. Synonyms

Select the word from the list that has the most similar meaning to the word in **bold**.

Chronicle	newspaper	report	ongoing	trumpet	herald
Verbose	diffuse	slim	quiet	long	loud
Prestige	disregard	cachet	humility	strong	weak
Wane	grow	extend	brighten	rise	abate
Attack	guard	surrender	war	maul	fire

3. Missing words

Choose the best word to complete the sentences.

Karen and Colin were (1) _____ (exited, excited, exciting) to be visiting the beach. Their mother had promised that they would be able to have a picnic lunch and that they would be (2) _____ (played, play, playing) games in the afternoon. The weather was bright and warm and both Karen and Colin were looking (3) _____ (foreward, forward, backwards) to swimming in the sea. Karen had (4) _____ (bought, brought, bringing) her new swimming costume which was covered in red and yellow flowers. Colin thought it would be (5) _____ (neccessary, neccesary, necessary) to choose somewhere to sit that was away from the water so that his sandcastle would not get washed away. It was definitely going to be a fun day.

Test 34

1. Fill in the missing words

Choose the most appropriate word from the list available to complete the following passage. Two of the words will not be needed.

| breathe | exists | absorb | contains | melted | dissolved | produced |

In the natural order of life there _____ a carbon dioxide cycle; that is, although the total amount in the air remains almost the same it is continually being _____ and used by various forms of life. Animals _____ in oxygen and turn some of this into carbon dioxide on breathing out. Carbon dioxide is also made by burning anything which _____ carbon, such as coal, wood, paper or petrol. Carbon dioxide is used up in many ways including the feeding of green plants, being _____ in the oceans and being absorbed by rocks.

2. Antonyms

Select the word from the list that has the most opposite meaning to the word in **bold**.

Foil	nullify	elude	balk	facilitate	cover
Extant	alive	angle	instant	current	gone
Derivative	original	offshoot	wave	constable	officer
Tirade	praise	invective	diatribe	ranting	sell
Wily	sly	cagey	frank	thin	fat

3. **Missing letters**

Fill in the missing letters to complete the words.

Instead of worrying about the o/ /t/ /o/m/ of a marathon race or training run, it is better to focus on the process and the i/n/ /i/v/ / /u/a/l steps that need to be taken to get to the end. For example, think about /e/t/ /i/ /g to the next street corner or mile marker in a race or up the next hill. That way you r/e/ /a/ /n focus on the present and stop worrying about the final result.

Test 35

1. Fill in the missing words

Choose the most appropriate word from the list available to complete the following passage. Two of the words will not be needed.

known	imaginary	understood	mean	gazes	represent	hewn

Sphinx is the Greek word for an _____ animal with a lion's body and a human or animal head. Statues of sphinxes in Egypt used to _____ the king or a god. The best _____ example is the one at Giza. This was made during the Old Kingdom of Egypt. It is about 20 metres tall and 73 metres long and is partly _____ from the natural rock and partly built of cut stone. It _____ eastwards across the River Nile towards Cairo.

2. Synonyms

Select the word from the list that has the most similar meaning to the word in **bold**.

Frail	infirm	strong	firm	pass	graduate
Fastidious	choosy	uncouth	uncover	slowly	stylish
Exquisite	outer	entrance	elegant	scruffy	vagabond
Vexation	joke	agitation	delight	joy	trick
Crude	polite	quiet	rude	petrol	diesel

3. Idioms

Match the idiom in **bold** to its meaning.

Call it a day	a. Get out of control
Break a leg	b. Stop working on something
Get out of hand	c. Don't be so critical
Cut someone some slack	d. Good luck
Speak of the devil	e. The person you were talking about appeared

Test 36

1. Antonyms

Select the word from the list that has the most opposite meaning to the word in bold.

Equilibrium	serenity	stability	imbalance	symmetry	algebra
Exhume	exhale	resurrect	disinter	reveal	bury
Deny	ratify	oppose	refute	forgo	lie
Liberal	flexible	radical	limited	free	open
Blame	acquit	admonish	ascribe	indict	chide

2. Idioms

Match the idiom in **bold** to its meaning.

Pull yourself together	a. To understand something complicated
To make matters worse	b. He's just like his father
Wrap your head around something	c. He has more important things to consider first
He has bigger fish to fry	d. Make a problem worse
He's a chip off the old block	e. Calm down

3. Missing letters

Fill in the missing letters to complete the words.

You don't have to be a bodybuilder or a sports scientist to know that protein is a/s/s/ /c/ /a/t/ /d with muscles and strength. Dissect a muscle and you'll find it consists almost /n/t/ /r/ /l/y of protein. As far as your training is concerned, protein does not have a major role on energy p/ /o/ /u/c/ /i/o/ but it is part of the structure of every cell in the body. Sufficient /i/e/ /a/ /y protein is essential for normal body maintenance and r/ /p/ /i/ /i/n/g/ muscle tissue.

Test 37

1. Antonyms

Select the word from the list that has the most opposite meaning to the word in bold.

Ostentatious	poor	garish	gaudy	jaunty	modest
Internal	outer	within	hidden	enclosed	taken
Succinct	pithy	blunt	outside	curt	lengthy
Absolve	forgive	pardon	relieve	wealthy	accuse
Oblivious	deaf	awake	blind	awkward	alive

2. Synonyms

Select the word from the list that has the most similar meaning to the word in **bold**.

Mediation	argument	control	redeem	contention	negotiation
Periphery	inner	diameter	fringe	radius	core
Ailment	medication	infirmary	diet	malady	treatment
Curt	polite	concise	wordy	civil	trade
Curb	restraint	opening	middle	core	fragment

3. Homophones and Homographs

Homographs are two words that are spelt the same but have different meanings.
Homophones are two words that sound the same but have different meanings and spellings.

From the list below, fill in the blanks. The first one has been done for you.

desert	discount	produce	pour	poor

1. They walked for hours across the hot ____desert____ in search of water.

2. She chose that shop because they had a _____ on her favourite sweets.

3. Tom tried to _____ his best drawing to date for the competition.

4. The greengrocer had his best _____ at the front of the store.

5. Cathy tried not to _____ Paul's suggestion when making her decision.

6. She had to _____ the milk carefully to avoiding spilling any.

7. He was _____ because he had too many bills and not enough money.

8. "Don't _____ me!" she cried, as he walked away.

Test 38

1. Fill in the missing words

Choose the most appropriate word from the list available to complete the following passage. Two of the words will not be needed.

| realities | remote | elected | Vatican | stance | discarded | opposed |

In 1878, Leo XIII was _____ pope following the death of Pius IX. The new pope, more a man of the world with a greater understanding of the _____ of political life, faced difficult problems in Italy and beyond. At first he remained as _____ to the Italian State as his predecessor but he came to raise that self-imposed political isolation risked making the Church even more _____ from the everyday lives of Italians. He gradually changed his _____ and allowed Catholics to become more directly involved in politics.

2. Idioms

Match the idiom in **bold** to its meaning.

Look before you leap	a. Very busy
Shape up or ship out	b. It's too late
Snowed under	c. Take only calculated risks
That ship has sailed	d. In good health
Fit as a fiddle	e. Work better or leave

3. Antonyms

Select the word from the list that has the most opposite meaning to the word in **bold**.

Zephyr	horse	meek	mild	tornado	wizard
Dally	stroll	hasten	dress	stop	commence
Progress	forward	advance	foreward	cease	regression
Umbrage	chagrin	ire	pique	professor	harmony
Henpecked	cowardly	assertive	floating	painful	weak

Test 39

1. Antonyms

Select the word from the list that has the most opposite meaning to the word in bold.

Minor	drill	petty	slight	trivial	major
Concurrent	confluent	mutual	divergent	joining	historical
Distant	adjacent	isolated	remote	past	local
Frigid	frosty	glacial	hard	friendly	awake
Aloof	interested	indifferent	above	apart	below

2. Fill in the missing words

Choose the most appropriate word from the list available to complete the following passage. Two of the words will not be needed.

other	material	light	gas	dark	average	visible

A typical galaxy may be anything from 6,000 to 60,000 _____ years across and may contain a thousand million stars or more. Our own galaxy is called the Milky Way and it is larger than the _____ galaxy, in fact it contains around a hundred thousand million stars. Besides stars, many galaxies contain a great deal of _____ in the form of fine dust and gases. Sometimes the light from hot glowing _____ outshines the stars in a galaxy. Apart from the Milky Way, three other galaxies are _____ to the naked eye. They are called Andromeda, the large Magellanic Cloud and the small Magellanic Cloud.

3. Synonyms

Select the word from the list that has the most similar meaning to the word in **bold**.

Trident	stride	purpose	harpoon	fork	judge
Feign	foreign	alien	local	natural	fabricate
Kiosk	fob	lock	keyhole	rancid	booth
Staunch	flexible	stalwart	weak	moving	slim
Blemish	flaw	clarity	adornment	strength	embellishment

Test 40

1. Synonyms

Select the word from the list that has the most similar meaning to the word in **bold**.

Chaos	galaxy	theory	partial	whole	havoc
Canine	horse	cat	dog	fish	monkey
Sever	extreme	likely	harsh	cut	tie
Cancel	create	veto	summon	advise	discuss
Allocation	taken	occupied	whole	department	quota

2. Idioms

Match the idiom in **bold** to its meaning.

Cut the mustard	a. He's crazy
Go down in flames	b. No matter what
He's off his rocker	c. You'll make mistakes if you rush something
Haste makes waste	d. Do a good job
Come rain or shine	e. To fail spectacularly

3. Odd one out

Four of the words in the list are linked in some way. Mark the word that is not linked, as shown in the example.

Example: dove   crow   ~~eat~~   magpie   eagle

1.   dollar   pound   money   euro   yen
2.   yacht   ship   canoe   ocean   dinghy
3.   lunch   eat   dinner   supper   breakfast
4.   arm   liver   kidney   heart   skin
5.   cheddar   brie   stilton   cracker   edam

Test 41

1. Antonyms

Select the word from the list that has the most opposite meaning to the word in bold.

Veer	bend	depart	view	deviate	straighten
Pompous	humble	bombastic	bloated	imperious	square
Bland	lively	insipid	tedious	tame	banal
Orthodox	devout	unconventional	conformist	religious	vicar
Volatile	erratic	lees	stable	deposits	fickle

2. Fill in the missing words

Choose the most appropriate word from the list available to complete the following passage. Two of the words will not be needed.

kingdom	defend	pottery	depicted	fate	needlework	invade

On October 14 1066 a battle was fought that decided the _____ of England, for by nightfall that day King Harold had been killed, his army defeated and William of Normandy had won a _____. The battle became known as the Battle of Hastings. William had been preparing to _____ England all through the summer, for he claimed that he and not King Harold, was the rightful heir of Edward the Confessor. The Battle of Hastings is _____ on the Bayeux Tapestry which is a famous piece of _____ produced during the time of William the Conqueror.

3. Missing letters

Fill in the missing letters to complete the words.

The human heart is pear-shaped and m/ /s/c/ /l/a/ . It pumps blood around the human body. The heart is at the centre of the /a/r/ /i/o/ /a/s/c/ /l/a/r system. The chief tasks of the cardiovascular system are to carry o/ / /g/ /n from the lungs and food materials from the organs of digestion and to remove waste products from the tissues. The heart is like a pumping station and the /r/t/ /r/i/ /s , veins and capillaries all interconnect with it. Oxygenated blood /e/a/ /e/ the heart and de-oxygenated blood is returned to the heart.

Test 42

1. Fill in the missing words

Choose the most appropriate word from the list available to complete the following passage. Two of the words will not be needed.

| justice | custom | obtained | priest | penance | distributed | ceremony |

The first day of Lent is called Ash Wednesday because in the early days of the Church, sinners did public _____ on that day by attending services dressed in sack-cloths and having ashes scattered over their heads by the priest. Later the _____ was extended to the entire congregation. The _____ is still held in a simpler version in the Roman Catholic Church. The ashes are sprinkled with holy water, the _____ then presses his thumb into the mixture and draws a cross on the forehead of each member of the congregation. The ashes used are _____ by burning the palms which were blessed the previous year on Palm Sunday.

2. Synonyms

Select the word from the list that has the most similar meaning to the word in **bold**.

Occult	average	mystical	above	higher	society
Weld	separate	metallic	disconnect	shorten	fuse
Marriage	antagonism	failure	harmony	matrimony	singular
Formidable	trivial	daunting	calm	feeble	worktop
Dialect	language	phone	call	shout	deceased

3. Idioms

Match the idiom in **bold** to its meaning.

Curiosity killed the cat	a. They're very alike
Have your head in the clouds	b. Hear news of something secret
Get wind of something	c. He can't make up his mind
He's sitting on the fence	d. Stop asking questions
Like two peas in a pod	e. Not be concentrating

Test 43

1. Antonyms

Select the word from the list that has the most opposite meaning to the word in bold.

Superfluous	useful	excessive	expendable	great	higher
Simple	daily	elementary	transparent	complicated	rare
Cloudy	opaque	foggy	distinct	sunny	muddle
Modern	obsolete	current	stylish	novel	apt
Submissive	meek	resistent	obedient	passive	under

2. Homophones and Homographs

Homographs are two words that are spelt the same but have different meanings.
Homophones are two words that sound the same but have different meanings and spellings.

From the list below, fill in the blanks. The first one has been done for you.

| idol | object | refuse | idle | tear |

1. Listening to my ___idol___ singing makes me so happy.

2. She could always _____ to tell him if he asked her for the details.

3. Katy liked to be busy, she could not stand to be _____.

4. He wondered what the _____ was on the side of the road.

5. There was a _____ in her dress after she caught it on the gate.

6. "I _____ to being spoken to in that way!" he said indignantly.

7. The workmen came to collect the _____ on Wednesdays.

8. A _____ ran down her cheek as she waved goodbye.

3. Odd one out

Four of the words in the list are linked in some way. Mark the word that is not linked, as shown in the example.

Example: dove   crow   ~~cat~~   magpie   eagle

1.   kid   puppy   kitten   foal   horse
2.   yurt   yogurt   teepee   wigwam   tent
3.   fork   knife   spoon   chopsticks   plate
4.   dawdle   amble   loiter   hurry   stroll
5.   stem   petal   leaf   tree   root

Test 44

1. Antonyms

Select the word from the list that has the most opposite meaning to the word in bold.

Cursory	random	superficial	brief	detailed	polite
Uniform	orderly	disorderly	constant	dress	stable
Capability	capacity	potential	means	inability	order
Covert	candid	hidden	privy	private	mission
Former	earlier	latter	bygone	shapely	after

2. Synonyms

Select the word from the list that has the most similar meaning to the word in **bold**.

Abhor	admire	like	similar	detest	approve
Trivial	paltry	major	essential	question	quiz
Juvenile	mature	old	experienced	formative	criminal
Coax	repel	cajole	repulse	disgust	trick
Aperture	agreement	camera	closing	harbour	chasm

3. Idioms

Match the idiom in **bold** to its meaning.

Let sleeping dogs lie	a. Run very fast
Run like the wind	b. Both people are responsible
It takes two to tango	c. Work quickly, time is a valuable resource
Jump on the bandwagon	d. Stop discussing an issue
Time is money	e. Follow a trend

Test 45

1. Synonyms

Select the word from the list that has the most similar meaning to the word in **bold**.

Jingoistic	misanthropic	traitorous	divided	triage	loyal
Odyssey	excursion	fantastic	outrageous	simple	stationary
Brood	ignore	consider	neglect	singular	lonesome
Swivel	wheel	pivot	track	circular	straight
Wit	turn	shaft	crevice	satire	seriousness

2. Homophones and Homographs

Homographs are two words that are spelt the same but have different meanings.
Homophones are two words that sound the same but have different meanings and spellings.

From the list below, fill in the blanks. The first one has been done for you.

| cell | evening | sell | project | wind |

1. The prisoner was kept in his ___cell___ until 4pm.

2. They went for a walk in the _____ to watch the fireworks.

3. The waves were _____ out around the boat.

4. The _____ was coming together well and would soon be finished.

5. Sarah tried to _____ up the toy but feared it might be broken.

6. Colin could feel the _____ on his face as he ran around the track.

7. Simon tried to _____ the javelin as far as possible to win first place.

8. If I can _____ 300 per week I can break even.

3. Antonyms

Select the word from the list that has the most opposite meaning to the word in **bold**.

Winsome	appealing	cute	absorbing	displeasing	thin
Spurious	phoney	contrived	pirate	spinning	valid
Sobriety	intemperance	continence	moderation	audacious	lofty
Scurrilous	salacious	decent	lewd	hurrying	slowly
Reprobate	moral	foul	recover	resell	lewd

Test 46

1. Antonyms

Select the word from the list that has the most opposite meaning to the word in bold.

Grieve	lament	rejoice	regret	bold	later
Forte	castle	aptitude	strength	weakness	talent
Apt	unlikely	liable	given	prone	upright
Appreciate	enhance	depreciate	gain	improve	dislike
Tame	curb	pacify	restrain	agitate	domestic

2. Fill in the missing words

Choose the most appropriate word from the list available to complete the following passage. Two of the words will not be needed.

hunters	daily	tablelands	simpler	success	people	ceremonies

In the southwest of the United States of America, there is an area of high _____, deep canyons and rich red sand. This is where the Navaho Indians live. For these _____, magic is a part of everyday life, just as it was for Stone Age man thousands of years ago. The Navahos use magic in _____ to bring them rain, to grow their crops, to drive away evil spirits and to cure illness. The magic of Stone Age man was much _____. It began with dances or drawings for _____ when hunting animals for food.

3. Synonyms

Select the word from the list that has the most similar meaning to the word in **bold**.

Emulate	neglect	imitate	encourage	soften	delay
Ambiguous	clear	large	dubious	determined	known
Dogmatic	fanatical	willing	yielding	amenable	canine
Restive	Obedient	jittery	calm	collected	sleeping
Joust	joke	agreement	bout	sword	dagger

Test 47

1. Fill in the missing words

Choose the most appropriate word from the list available to complete the following passage. Two of the words will not be needed.

| dangerous | stomachs | known | hydrogen | safe | oxygen | mouths |

Acids are among the most useful and sometimes the most _____ of chemical substances. Hydrochloric acid, for example, is a deadly poison, but if people did not have a small quantity of this acid in their _____ they would not be able to digest their food properly. At one time it was thought that all acids contained _____ but this was found to be incorrect. It is now known that all acids contain _____, which is given off when metals are dissolved in an acid. Acids that come from plants or animals are _____ as organic acids.

2. Idioms

Match the idiom in **bold** to its meaning.

Weather the storm	a. This isn't over yet
A dime a dozen	b. The worse possible situation
Give you the benefit of the doubt	c. Go through something difficult
It ain't over till the fat lady sings	d. Something common
A perfect storm	e. Trust what you say

3. **Odd one out**

Four of the words in the list are linked in some way. Mark the word that is not linked, as shown in the example.

Example: dove   crow   ~~cat~~   magpie   eagle

1.   screen   keyboard   mouse   motherboard   desk
2.   boot   shoe   bonnet   seats   doors
3.   rock   disco   classical   grunge   classic
4.   sleet   snow   wind   hail   rain
5.   English   Japanese   France   Spanish   Portuguese

Test 48

1. Fill in the missing words

Choose the most appropriate word from the list available to complete the following passage. Two of the words will not be needed.

| skimp | isolate | preparatory | work | preparation | lock | area |

Thorough _____ is the key to successful decorating. If you neglect or _____ over the groundwork, the finished surface will always suffer. First, make ready the _____ to be decorated. Indoors, _____ the room where you will be working before preparing the surfaces. Most _____ work creates mess and dust which easily spreads to other areas. Wherever possible, clear out everything movable before you start work.

2. Synonyms

Select the word from the list that has the most similar meaning to the word in **bold**.

Warden	prisoner	hospital	prepare	initiate	caretaker
Rebuke	chide	approve	return	compliment	laud
Zeal	apathy	dullness	diligence	lethargy	pith
Zenith	base	utmost	base	depth	apex
Jeer	compliment	ridicule	praise	joke	flatter

3. Antonyms

Select the word from the list that has the most opposite meaning to the word in **bold**.

Proscribe	medical	doctor	allow	banish	exile
Obdurate	callous	firm	amenable	dogged	obtuse
Nadir	top	base	floor	king	pauper
Multifarious	assorted	homogenous	many	myriad	royal
Largesse	fund	alms	philanthropy	small	meanness

Test 49

1. Antonyms

Select the word from the list that has the most opposite meaning to the word in bold.

Averse	agreeable	hesitant	loath	hostile	left
Flout	defy	heed	mock	scorn	advertise
Reverence	esteem	disregard	admiration	piety	lowly
Envelop	surround	swaddle	release	letter	wrap
Bitter	angry	grateful	acidic	sour	tasty

2. Synonyms

Select the word from the list that has the most similar meaning to the word in **bold**.

Deride	flatter	scorn	compliment	travel	gain
Endurance	inability	apathy	lethargy	length	stamina
Axe	join	unite	unity	cancel	hire
Shrewd	idiotic	dull	canny	blunt	inept
Collaborator	enemy	foe	friend	partner	holder

3. Idioms

Match the idiom in **bold** to its meaning.

Add insult to injury	a. Very expensive
Costs an arm and a leg	b. Tell me what you're thinking
A picture is worth a 1000 words	c. To make a bad situation worse
Bite off more than you can chew	d. Take on something that you cannot finish
A penny for your thoughts	e. Better to show than tell

Test 50

1. Missing letters

Fill in the missing letters to complete the words in the boxes.

In 1069 William the Conqueror **c / e / / / b / / a / t / e / d** Christmas in York. It was three years since his **c / o / r / / n / / / i / o / n** as king of England, which had taken place at Westminster Abbey on Christmas Day 1066, just weeks after his **v / / c / / o / / y** at the Battle of Hastings. To celebrate the **a / n / / / v / e / r / / a / r / /** of his coronation, William had ordered that his crown and other **r / e / / / l / / a** be brought to York in order that he may wear them for the Christmas **f / / / t / / v / i / t / / e / s**.

2. Odd one out

Four of the words in the list are linked in some way. Mark the word that is not linked, as shown in the example.

Example: dove   crow   ~~cat~~   magpie   eagle

1.	ash	rowan	burn	willow	beech
2.	nose	wing	hold	eye	tail
3.	vast	spread	large	huge	immense
4.	helium	oxygen	tin	nitrogen	hydrogen
5.	Africa	Nigeria	Somalia	Chad	Morocco

3. Idioms

Match the idiom in **bold** to its meaning.

Give someone the cold shoulder	a. Slow down
Barking up the wrong tree	b. To ignore someone
Easy does it	c. Don't give up
Hang in there	d. Unwell
Under the weather	e. To be mistaken

Answers

Test 1

1. Antonyms

Background foreground
Commend criticise
Rear fore
Everyday rare
Muddled organised

2. Fill in the missing words

In the Middle Ages, jewels often had a religious **meaning**, for the art of making jewellery was carefully kept up in the monasteries. Jewels were used to **adorn** shrines, the **vestments** of the priest and the vessels used in church services. These were often made of gold and decorated with **precious** stones. Gradually, however, the making of jewellery became a **trade** as well as an art and jewels grew to be **looked** upon as part of costume.

3. Synonyms

Doomed fated
Genre category
Report announce
Binary double
Duplicate clone

4. Missing words

1. metal
2. than
3. temperature
4. brittle
5. rolled

Test 2

1. Fill in the missing words

Juno was the **name** the Romans gave to the queen of the gods and goddesses, whose **husband** was the supreme god Jupiter. Iris, **goddess** of the rainbow, was Juno's messenger and she was **attended** by the peacock who was said to have 100 eyes in his tail. She was queen of **Earth** as well as heaven and was the especial **protectress** of women who called upon her for help in their troubles.

2. Synonyms

Deplore	abhor
Detest	loathe
Startle	stun
Conceited	arrogant
Uproar	confusion

3. Idioms

Don't give up your day job	b	a. Get something exactly right
Every cloud has a silver lining	d	b. You're not very good at this
It's a piece of cake	c	c. It's easy
Once in a blue moon	e	d. Good things come after bad things
Hit the nail on the head	a	e. Rarely

4. Antonyms

Awake	dormant
Clean	soiled
Noteworthy	pedestrian
Secrete	reveal
Veto	approve

Test 3

1. Antonyms

Narrator	listener
Kind	cruel
Peripheral	central
Jolly	miserable
Vain	modest

2. **Fill in the missing words**

George III, who **succeeded** his grandfather in 1760, was 22 when he began his long reign. He had been **brought** up as an Englishman and was greatly interested in Britain and its empire. However his policy was not always **successful** and he was largely responsible for the loss of the American colonies. Later in his **reign** he suffered from fits of madness and his eldest son ruled for him, with the title of Prince Regent. When the Prince Regent became George IV, on his father's **death** in 1820, he was already 58 and had fallen into an extravagant and **rowdy** way of life.

3. **Homophones and Homographs**

1. The first time he went fishing he managed to catch a **bass**.
2. You need a **bat** to play cricket.
3. Their weapons were the **bow** and arrow and stones.
4. Would you like a **break** from all that hard work you've been doing?
5. Try to **brake** gently when you're driving if the roads are wet.
6. Joan cannot play the **bass** guitar.
7. It was dark outside when Mary noticed the **bat** flying around.
8. The child was thrilled he could tie a knot and a **bow**.

Test 4

1. **Antonyms**

Murmur	shout
Alarm	assure
Contradict	affirm
Boost	undermine
Perfect	corrupt

2. **Fill in the missing words**

Lantern fish generally live in the **deeper** parts of the oceans. There the water is cold and dark, for **sunlight** cannot reach far below the surface. Lantern fish are so **named** because they have luminous spots on their bodies which give out light. It is likely that a sudden flash of these lights is used to **frighten** or dazzle a pursuer. Some lantern fish have shining dots scattered over the lower parts of their bodies and others have a large spot or **streak** that gives off light above and below the base of the tail, while at least one has a large spot at the end of the **snout**, like the headlight of a car.

3. **Idioms**

Ignorance is bliss	b	a. Events have momentum and can build up
Go on a wild goose chase	e	b. You're better off not knowing
A snowball effect	a	c. Destroy relationships
Burn bridges	c	d. Perfect
As right as rain	d	e. To do something pointless

Test 5

1. **Antonyms**

Compliant	inflexible
Hearty	weak
Moving	stationary
Dissuade	encourage
End	commence

2. **Fill in the missing words**

Camellia flower blight can be easily **confused** with frost damage or grey mould. Frost **damage** is normally confined to the edges of the petals or, in severe cases, affects the whole flower at once. Grey **mould** can cause similar brown flecks, but will also produce fuzzy, grey growth under **humid** conditions. Camellia flower blight has the **distinctive**, diagnostic feature of a ring of white fungal growth visible around the **base** of the petals.

3. **Synonyms**

Brag	crow
Brawl	tussle
Range	array
Deploy	use
Showy	ornate

4. **Missing words**

1. warm
2. animals
3. alpaca
4. grow
5. coarse

Test 6

1. Fill in the missing words

Jamaica is one of the most **important** islands in the Caribbean Sea and is an independent **country** of the Commonwealth of Nations. It is roughly the same size as Northern Ireland and **lies** about 100 miles south of Cuba. Somewhat **farther** distant to the east across the Jamaica Channel is the island of Hispaniola, now divided into two countries, Haiti and the Dominican Republic. Jamaica is a very mountainous **island**. A **ridge** of high land runs along the island, rising in the east to the Blue Mountains with a peak of 7402ft, the highest in the West Indies.

2. Synonyms

Counsel	advise
Mock	deride
Artificial	bogus
Burrow	delve
Clog	block

3. Idioms

Once bitten, twice shy	b	a.	We agree
On cloud nine	d	b.	You're more cautious a second time
We see eye to eye	a	c.	Everything is going wrong at once
Through thick and thin	e	d.	Very happy
When it rains it pours	c	e.	In good times and in bad times

4. Antonyms

Sanction	oppose
Arduous	facile
Total	part
Useless	valuable
Vacant	engaged

Test 7

1.   Antonyms

Remiss	careful
Sell	purchase
Sane	irrational
Grip	release
Credible	doubtful

2.   Fill in the missing words

The mackerel is a **handsome**, streamlined fish whose second dorsal fin and the anal fin are divided into a number of small separate **finlets** above and below the tail. These control the flow of water over the tail as the fish swims, so that **eddies** do not form and slow the fish down. That is why the mackerel and its **relatives**, the bonitos and tunnies, are among the fastest of fish and are able to move quickly for long periods. They **roam** the ocean in great **shoals**, feeding on the small fish, crustacea and other creatures near the surface.

3.   Synonyms

Pragmatic	efficient
Clothe	drape
Vista	landscape
Token	symbol
Depression	deflation

Test 8

1.   Antonyms

Persuade	deter
Boom	recession
Havoc	calm
Factual	fictitious
Contradict	endorse

2. **Fill in the missing words**

Mamba is the name given to a group of **slender**, active snakes some of which live in trees. They are closely **related** to the cobras and are often called tree-cobras. Because of the strength of their **poison**, mambas are among the most dangerous of poisonous snakes. They are found in tropical and southern Africa. There are several **species** of mambas. Some are bright leaf-green in colour which makes them very difficult to see when they are **coiled** among the leaves of a tree. These are called green mambas. Others are a dark, gun-metal grey and are **commonly** known as black mambas.

3. **Odd one out**

1.	division	~~equation~~	subtraction	addition	multiplication
2.	house	flat	~~car~~	bungalow	mansion
3.	eyes	nose	~~legs~~	mouth	ears
4.	north	~~below~~	south	west	east
5.	five	seven	eleven	~~half~~	twelve

Test 9

1. **Fill in the missing words**

The maple family includes the **sycamore**. Like the sycamore, the field maple has **winged** seeds which are carried by the wind. The field maple is **native** to Great Britain. Maple leaves, which contain **sugar**, are glossy and are divided round their edges into five parts. They used to be collected as food for **cattle**, as cows enjoyed them. The yellow-green flowers, which open in May and June, stand up in little **clusters**.

2. **Synonyms**

Shop boutique
Avoid dodge
Authenticate substantiate
Abundance profusion
Clemency mercy

3. **Idioms**

A blessing in disguise	e	a. Better to arrive late than not at all
Better late than never	a	b. Unwell
So far so good	d	c. I have no idea
Your guess is as good as mine	c	d. Things are going well so far
Under the weather	b	e. A good thing that seemed bad at first

4. **Antonyms**

Circumvent confront
Civilized primitive
Chronological random
Compliance resistance
Dominant inconspicuous

Test 10

1. **Antonyms**

Extrovert introvert
Minimum maximum
Fidelity enmity
Harmony discord
Valuable worthless

2. **Fill in the missing words**

Diesel engines, which work in the same way as those of motor **buses** and lorries, came **rapidly** into use for driving ships after World War I. Those used in big ships are generally large, heavy engines with anything up to eight **cylinders**. Smaller ships may use high-speed diesels **connected** to the propeller shafts either by mechanical **gearing** or, in diesel-electric ships, by using alternators and electric motors like those for turbo-electric drive. Diesel engines are **economical**, giving more power for each ton of fuel burnt than any other kind.

3. Odd one out

1. piano   ~~stool~~   flute   trumpet   clarinet
2. ~~love~~   hatred   fear   greed   anger
3. dog   cat   monkey   ~~dragon~~   horse
4. mother   ~~friend~~   daughter   son   father
5. shoe   sandal   boot   ~~glove~~   trainer

Test 11

1. Antonyms

Popular   obscure
Resolute   complacent
Zany   serious
Unkempt   ordered
Permanent   ephemeral

2. Fill in the missing words

The flower is the **reproductive** structure of flowering plants, which gives rise to seeds and fruit. The flower provides a **mechanism** for pollen from the male part of the flower to **fertilise** the egg cells in the female part of the flower. The flowers may develop or be constructed in such a way as to encourage cross-pollination between different flowers, or **permit** self-pollination within the same flower. Many plants have **evolved** to produce large, colourful flowers that are attractive to animal pollinators, others have evolved to produce dull, scentless flowers that are **pollinated** by the wind.

3. Homophones and Homographs

1. After making bread she had ____**flour**____ all over her apron.
2. She asked him to **row** across the lake as she felt tired.
3. He could not afford a motorbike so bought a cheaper **moped** instead.
4. The groom wore a beautiful **flower** in his lapel on his wedding day.
5. She was very miserable and **moped** around the house all day.
6. She did not want to **row** with him so agreed with his suggestion.
7. The book describes his **entrance** into politics.
8. The thief gained **entrance** via the backdoor.

Test 12

1. Synonyms

Family	clan
Altitude	elevation
Vain	arrogant
Antagonist	enemy
Fake	hoax

2. Fill in the missing words

Cheese is distinguished by its flavour: **bland**, like Edam, or powerfully strong, like Provolone. It is also **categorised** according to texture: fresh, soft, semi-hard or hard. Cheese may be identified partly by the **formation** of the rind. The rind protects the cheese's interior and allows it to **ripen** properly. Apart from those with a manufactured wax coating, such as Edam or Gouda, there are those with a dry or natural **rind**, such as Stilton. Some cheeses are bathed in a brine solution. This hardens the rind and **improves** the flavour of the body.

3. Idioms

The best of both worlds	b	a. Doing a good job
Hang in there	e	b. Where either of two choices are advantageous
On the ball	a	c. To joke with someone
Pull someone's leg	c	d. It's raining heavily
It's raining cats and dogs	d	e. Don't give up

Test 13

1. Antonyms

Beleaguer	assist
Logical	irrational
Destitute	affluent
Idle	active
Absurd	sane

2. Fill in the missing words

From the earliest times, man has been a **carnivorous** animal. Because meat provides so much **protein** and essential vitamins, early people could spend less of their time eating and could successfully turn their **energies** to activities which in time placed them above their peers. Meat was, from the beginning, equated with life and early hunting was designed to supply a **plentiful** amount of animals. Though today there is a reappraisal of the importance of meat in the diet - whether its drawbacks like cholesterol and high price **outweigh** its value as a protein provider, or, in the case of vegetarians, an **ethical** consideration - meat is still one of the most expensive items on the shopping list.

3. Odd one out

1.	lake	~~forest~~	ocean	river	sea
2.	happy	elated	cheerful	~~grumpy~~	joyous
3.	beef	pork	chicken	~~peas~~	lamb
4.	apple	banana	~~asparagus~~	peach	plum
5.	silver	gold	tin	~~paper~~	lead

Test 14

1. Antonyms

Release	restraint
Evict	admit
Evoke	repress
Linger	advance
Commence	stop

2. Fill in the missing words

The educational **thought** of our time has been chiefly **directed** toward the improvement of city school systems. So we hear of the great schools in London, Manchester, Birmingham and Edinburgh **amongst** other places; but we have yet to hear of a single county or village of rural population, the excellence of whose schools entitles them to national **repute**. The emphasis of our thought has been placed long and hard on **urban** schools at the expense of the rural schools. It is time to change the **emphasis** of our ideas and to consider the necessities of the rural schools.

3. Synonyms

Inane	daft
Merciful	lenient
Considerate	generous
Frank	blunt
Legitimate	lawful

Test 15

1.   Antonyms

Barbaric	cultured
Wholly	partially
Obtuse	intelligent
Plunge	rise
Decelerate	accelerate

2.   Fill in the missing words

The range of conifers available is so wide that there is an **option** for almost every space. You can choose from **evergreen** or deciduous conifers; blue, green or yellow foliage; and a wide range of growth habits. The speed at which a conifer will grow can often be **estimated** by looking at the size of the previous season's extension growth; otherwise look at the plant's growth habit with a view to **pruning** or shaping. For example, a pine or Abies has obvious branch **joints** where pruning cuts can be made **tactfully** and without spoiling the look of the plant. By contrast, something more globular and rounded in shape, such as Cryptomeria, is usually best if just left to grow.

3.   Synonyms

Gregarious	affable
Compassion	empathy
Coy	bashful
Fatal	mortal
Override	annul

Test 16

1.   Fill in the missing words

Porcelain is the **aristocrat** of clay bodies, the most highly refined of all clay body types. It is rarely found as a natural body but is a **compound** of a blend of kaolins, china clays, ball clays and feldspars. Porcelain's characteristic **properties** include: an extreme fineness of grain structure, hardness and toughness when fired, resistance to acids and **translucency**. Its colour is usually white or blue-white when fired. Porcelain **products** are usually thin-walled and should be handled with care as they are extremely **delicate**.

2. Idioms

Give someone the cold shoulder	b	a. Make people feel more comfortable
ABowtin ice	e	b. Ignore someone
Break the ice	a	c. You're just as bad as they are
It takes one to know one	c	d. Fix the problem now or it will get worse later
A stitch in time saves nine	d	e. If you make another mistake there will be trouble

3. Homophones and Homographs

1. He knew he would **die** if he drank the poison.
2. She held the duckling in her hand and could feel its soft **down**.
3. Oliver could only just see the small key it was so **minute**.
4. "Wait a **minute**!" he shouted, "I'm just coming."
5. If you park on a restricted road you risk being charged a **fine**.
6. Jane would have to **dye** her blouse if she wanted to change the colour.
7. He knew everything would be **fine** if he arrived on time.
8. He looked **down** the well and could just see the water below.

Test 17

1. Antonyms

Advanced	behind
Stout	slight
Annul	enact
Upset	order
Cajole	repulse

2. Odd one out

1.	walk	jog	run	~~sit~~	shuffle
2.	tango	rumba	waltz	~~run~~	samba
3.	pencil	~~paper~~	pen	crayon	chalk
4.	milk	cheese	yogurt	~~bread~~	butter
5.	arrow	spear	dagger	~~shield~~	knife

3. Missing words

1. enter
2. queen
3. started
4. chooses
5. hangs

Test 18

1. Antonyms

Augment	abridge
Trail	lead
Sound	unstable
Strapping	attenuated
Pollute	clean

2. Synonyms

Deputy	ambassador
Deed	action
Cancel	abort
Deplore	mourn
Flamboyant	dazzling

3. Odd one out

1. how — cow — ~~low~~ — now — pow
2. Earth — Mercury — ~~Sun~~ — Venus — Jupiter
3. September — April — June — ~~January~~ — November
4. March — ~~September~~ — July — January — December
5. jacket — trousers — shoes — ~~cloth~~ — hat

Test 19

1. Fill in the missing words

As a rule of thumb, when it comes to beef, those parts of the animal at the top, along the centre back to the rump end, are the **tenderest** and that makes them well-suited to fast cooking methods such as roasting, **grilling** and frying. The **shoulders** and lower legs of the cow, the parts that are worked hardest when the animal is alive, **yield** up tougher cuts which are usually cheaper and blessed with lots of flavour, but they require long and **gentle** cooking. When roasting beef, the larger the joint the better. Forerib is the best of all, but **sirloin** comes a close second.

2. Idioms

An apple a day keeps the doctor away	b	a. Everything, the whole way
Bolt from the blue	d	b. Eating nutritious food is good for you
Calm before the storm	e	c. The issue that people are avoiding
The whole nine yards	a	d. Something that happened without warning
The elephant in the room	c	e. It's fine now but something bad is coming

3. Synonyms

Wharf	dock
Thwart	impede
Bogus	spurious
Graft	work
Eloquence	fluency

Test 20

1. Antonyms

Harmless	dangerous
Prodigal	careful
Swift	slow
Lean	fatty
Rural	urban

2.   Synonyms

Revere   admire
Gauge   assess
Impair   diminish
Judicious   astute
Rhetoric   oratory

3.   Missing words

1. process
2. together
3. equals
4. remainder
5. dash

Test 21

1.   Antonyms

Concise   wordy
Taut   loose
Disencumber   burden
Separate   unite
Climb   slump

2.   Fill in the missing words

The wild crab apple is the **ancestor** of all apples. It is a native tree of Britain and is common in woods and **hedgerows** everywhere except the north of Scotland. It **seldom** grows to a greater height than thirty feet. The shape of the crab apple varies a great deal, but the branches are usually spreading and slightly drooping and the twigs are **spiny**. The rose-pink, sometimes pinkish-white flowers appear just before the leaves in April and look lovely as they are **borne** in clusters on short shoots. The apples ripen in October. They are small and may be either yellow or red. Whichever colour they are they are much too **bitter** to eat, but can be made into excellent jelly.

3.   Odd one out

1. banana   apple   ~~almond~~   plum   orange
2. ~~listen~~ swim   walk   run   climb
3. drill   hammer   screwdriver   ~~wood~~   pliers
4. ant   fly   beetle   ~~dog~~   wasp
5. bake   ~~peel~~   fry   roast   grill

118

Test 22

1. Fill in the missing words

Michelangelo was born in Italy in 1475. His father was a **magistrate** and proud of his noble ancestry. The family moved to Florence shortly after Michelangelo was born and he was placed in the care of a **foster** mother who lived just outside the city. Michelangelo's mother died when he was six years old and his father **remarried**. From a young age he was **determined** to be a sculptor but his father thought this was not a worthy **profession** for the son of a noble house. Despite this he went on to become one of the world's greatest artists. In 1501 he sculpted the famous statue of David from a **block** of marble that had been lying in a courtyard for a hundred years.

2. Synonyms

Emit — emanate
Eddy — vortex
Assumption — hunch
Omit — neglect
Cove — bay

3. Idioms

A storm in a teacup	b	a. That's true, I agree
To get bent out of shape	c	b. A big fuss about a small problem
You can say that again	a	c. To get upset
Go back to the drawing board	e	d. To not hold someone responsible for something
Let someone off the hook	d	e. Start all over again

Test 23

1. Fill in the missing words

I picked up the fuse and opened my lantern to get a light. Then I lit the **fuse** and made sure it was burning well. I raced back to the raft. Hans pushed off. At a safe distance from **shore** we waited. The **seconds** ticked by. Suddenly, the rock exploded. We stared into a **bottomless** pit. The sea swelled into a great wave and the raft **tossed** madly. We were thrown to the deck and there was no light. In the darkness the **roar** of water filled my ears. We had blown up a rock which blocked the entrance to a pit leading down to the centre of the Earth.

2. Synonyms

Snippet   fragment
Designate   nominate
Marginal   minor
Quaint   peculiar
Sect   faction

3. Idioms

It's not rocket science	d	a. It's too late
Miss the boat	a	b. My patience has run out
No pain no gain	e	c. To reveal a secret
That's the last straw	b	d. It's not complicated
Let the cat out of the bag	c	e. You have to work hard to get what you want

Test 24

1. Antonyms

Beautify   mar
Eschew   keep
Luminous   dull
Gloomy   hopeful
Dampen   dehydrate

2. Homophones and Homographs

1. After taking a tumble, Emma realised the **wound** on her leg was quite bad.
2. Jack **wound** the crown on his watch to change the time.
3. Carol read the **contract** before signing it.
4. But he had to **wave** his hand high if she was to notice him.
5. The surfer suddenly stood up and balanced on his board on the high **wave**.
6. "It was **our** fault" I said, "we didn't see him coming".
7. She was due to arrive on the **hour** but was running late.
8. Peter was worried he may **contract** the disease if he wasn't immunised.

3. **Odd one out**

1.	London	Dublin	Canberra	~~Newcastle~~	Paris
2.	helium	oxygen	hydrogen	~~aluminium~~	nitrogen
3.	stool	~~table~~	chair	bench	sofa
4.	England	France	~~Africa~~	Poland	Sweden
5.	guitar	viola	~~clarinet~~	violin	cello

Test 25

1. **Antonyms**

Permanent	temporary
Calibrate	destroy
Strife	agreement
Permit	prevent
Restrict	develop

2. **Synonyms**

Lurch	careen
Carp	quibble
Sporadic	irregular
Prune	clip
Ancillary	additional

3. **Missing words**

1. swallowing
2. form
3. anchoring
4. where
5. substance

Test 26

1. **Fill in the missing words**

There are many types of ponds to explore, even in busy towns and **cities**. Wherever water collects for any length of time, new life **springs** rapidly into being. You can test this fact for yourself by sinking a bowl into the ground and letting it fill **naturally** with rainwater. Before many days have passed, you will see that a green scum is beginning to cover the **surface**. This is called algae and it has grown from **spores** so tiny you cannot see them with the naked eye, you need a microscope. Algae gives off oxygen. All animals need oxygen to live so although this green scum may not look very attractive it is essential to **maintain** life in the water.

2. Odd one out

1. scarf   tie   necklace   collar   ~~sock~~
2. pongy   whiffy   smelly   ~~tasty~~   malodorous
3. did   had   were   ~~will~~   went
4. clown   ringmaster   ~~doctor~~   juggler   acrobat
5. stalls   balcony   auditorium   stage   ~~school~~

3. Antonyms

Flagrant	delicate
Insidious	sincere
Laconic	verbose
Vilify	flatter
Puerile	mature

Test 27

1. Antonyms

Strange	normal
Encourage	block
Enlarge	reduce
Liberate	detain
Impartial	prejudiced

2. Synonyms

Yearn	covet
Gradient	incline
Avid	ardent
Dormant	inert
Trench	gully

3. Missing letters

1. ancient
2. fortress
3. executed
4. historic
5. monument
6. guarded

Test 28

1. Antonyms

Break	juncture
Familiar	alien
Biased	impartial
Allay	incite
Just	corrupt

2. Idioms

Good things come to those who wait	d	a. Just barely
By the skin of your teeth	a	b. To make a mistake but to learn from it
Comparing apples to oranges	e	c. It's your decision
Live and learn	b	d. Be patient
The ball is in your court	c	e. Comparing two things that cannot be compared

3. Missing letters

1. breakfast
2. water
3. sweeten
4. becoming
5. special

Test 29

1. Idioms

Bite the bullet	c	a. Tell something briefly
Get your act together	e	b. Go to sleep
Hit the sack	b	c. To get something that is inevitable done
Make a long story short	a	d. Slow down
Easy does it	d	e. Work better

2. Odd one out

1. Mrs / Miss / ~~Master~~ / Madam / Ms
2. doctor / nurse / consultant / ~~solicitor~~ / surgeon
3. crow / eagle / ~~emu~~ / albatross / robin
4. depart / exit / withdraw / ~~arrive~~ / vacate
5. terrier / poodle / ~~siamese~~ / greyhound / collie

3. Antonyms

Noxious	sterile
Plethora	scarcity
Probity	corruption
Sanguine	pessimistic
Stolid	lively

Test 30

1. Fill in the missing words

Jupiter is the fifth planet from our Sun and is, by far, the **largest** planet in the solar system. It is more than twice as **massive** as all the other planets combined. Jupiter's stripes and swirls are actually cold, windy clouds of **ammonia** and water, floating in an atmosphere of hydrogen and helium. Jupiter's iconic Great Red Spot is a giant storm bigger than Earth that has **raged** for hundreds of years. Jupiter is **surrounded** by 79 known moons. Scientists are most interested in the four largest moons discovered by Galileo Galilei in 1610: Io, Europa, Ganymede and Callisto. Jupiter is named for the king of the **ancient** Roman gods.

2. Synonyms

Evaluate	appraise
Clause	passage
Rampant	flagrant
Sly	astute
Hospitable	friendly

3. Antonyms

Swarthy	light
Torpid	active
Rife	limited
Quixotic	cautious
Hapless	fortuitous

Test 31

1. Fill in the missing words

Over recent years, many of our once-common butterflies have **declined** dramatically in number due to increased development, agricultural intensification, habitat loss and **climate** change; for instance, the small tortoiseshell has decreased by a **massive** 80% in South East England since 1990. But butterflies do have a lifeline. Together, the 16 million gardens across the UK **form** an area for wildlife larger than all our National Nature Reserves. This patchwork of habitats helps our wildlife to move about freely, forming a vast living landscape that links **urban** green spaces with the wider countryside.

2. Synonyms

Gorge	devour
Flout	mock
Toll	levy
Truce	amnesty
Eerie	creepy

3. Homophones and Homographs

1. Jake took two **axes** with him to chop down the tree.
2. "What time of **night** do you call this young lady?" her father asked.
3. She always tied her hair in a **band.**
4. Six planets in our solar system rotate in the same direction on their **axes**.
5. She was **content** with the standard of her work.
6. Marion had never seen a **knight** before and was very impressed.
7. The **content** of the book disappointed Tom and he could not finish it.
8. Chris desperately wanted to sing in a **band** but he was tone deaf.

Test 32

1. Antonyms

Hard	vulnerable
Amass	divide
Composure	agitation
Complacent	troubled
Hoard	scatter

2. **Odd one out**

1. wink   stare   ~~pout~~   blink   see
2. ankle   wrist   elbow   knee   ~~bicep~~
3. femur   ulna   radius   scapula   ~~deltoid~~
4. meadow   pasture   ~~mountain~~   lea   field
5. gram   kilogram   ounce   ~~metre~~   ton

3. **Missing letters**

1. belongs
2. appearance
3. mimic
4. mountain
5. quarries

Test 33

1. **Antonyms**

Deteriorate	improve
Apathetic	caring
Local	alien
Dismantle	repair
Overlook	notice

2. **Synonyms**

Chronicle	report
Verbose	diffuse
Prestige	cachet
Wane	abate
Attack	maul

3. **Missing words**

1. excited
2. playing
3. forward
4. brought
5. necessary

Test 34

1. Fill in the missing words

In the natural order of life there **exists** a carbon dioxide cycle; that is, although the total amount in the air remains almost the same it is continually being **produced** and used by various forms of life. Animals **breathe** in oxygen and turn some of this into carbon dioxide on breathing out. Carbon dioxide is also made by burning anything which **contains** carbon, such as coal, wood, paper or petrol. Carbon dioxide is used up in many ways including the feeding of green plants, being **dissolved** in the oceans and being absorbed by rocks.

2. Antonyms

Foil	facilitate
Extant	gone
Derivative	original
Tirade	praise
Wily	frank

3. Missing letters

1. outcome
2. individual
3. getting
4. retain

Test 35

1. Fill in the missing words

Sphinx is the Greek word for an **imaginary** animal with a lion's body and a human or animal head. Statues of sphinxes in Egypt used to **represent** the king or a god. The best **known** example is the one at Giza. This was made during the Old Kingdom of Egypt. It is about 20 metres tall and 73 metres long and is partly **hewn** from the natural rock and partly built of cut stone. It **gazes** eastwards across the River Nile towards Cairo.

2. Synonyms

Frail	infirm
Fastidious	choosy
Exquisite	elegant
Vexation	agitation
Crude	rude

3. Idioms

Call it a day	b	a. Get out of control
Break a leg	d	b. Stop working on something
Get out of hand	a	c. Don't be so critical
Cut someone some slack	c	d. Good luck
Speak of the devil	e	e. The person you were talking about appeared

Test 36

1. Antonyms

Equilibrium imbalance
Exhume bury
Deny ratify
Liberal limited
Blame acquit

2. Idioms

Pull yourself together	e	a. To understand something complicated
To make matters worse	d	b. He's just like his father
Wrap your head around something	a	c. He has more important things to consider first
He has bigger fish to fry	c	d. Make a problem worse
He's a chip off the old block	b	e. Calm down

3. Missing letters

1. associated
2. entirely
3. production
4. dietary
5. repairing

Test 37

1.   Antonyms

Ostentatious	modest
Internal	outer
Succinct	lengthy
Absolve	accuse
Oblivious	awake

2.   Synonyms

Mediation	negotiation
Periphery	fringe
Ailment	malady
Curt	concise
Curb	restraint

3.   Homophones and Homographs

1. They walked for hours across the hot **desert** in search of water.
2. She chose that shop because they had a **discount** on her favourite sweets.
3. Tom tried to **produce** his best drawing to date for the competition.
4. The greengrocer had his best **produce** at the front of the store.
5. Cathy tried not to **discount** Paul's suggestion when making her decision.
6. She had to **pour** the milk carefully to avoiding spilling any.
7. He was **poor** because he had too many bills and not enough money.
8. "Don't **desert** me!" she cried, as he walked away.

Test 38

1.   Fill in the missing words

In 1878, Leo XIII was **elected** pope following the death of Pius IX. The new pope, more a man of the world with a greater understanding of the **realities** of political life, faced difficult problems in Italy and beyond. At first he remained as **opposed** to the Italian State as his predecessor but he came to realise that self-imposed political isolation risked making the Church even more **remote** from the everyday lives of Italians. He gradually changed his **stance** and allowed Catholics to become more directly involved in politics.

2. **Idioms**

Look before you leap	c	a. Very busy
Shape up or ship out	e	b. It's too late
Snowed under	a	c. Take only calculated risks
That ship has sailed	b	d. In good health
Fit as a fiddle	d	e. Work better or leave

3. **Antonyms**

Zephyr tornado
Dally hasten
Progress regression
Umbrage harmony
Henpecked assertive

Test 39

1. **Antonyms**

Minor major
Concurrent divergent
Distant adjacent
Frigid friendly
Aloof interested

2. **Fill in the missing words**

A typical galaxy may be anything from 6,000 to 60,000 **light** years across and may contain a thousand million stars or more. Our own galaxy is called the Milky Way and it is larger than the **average** galaxy, in fact it contains around a hundred thousand million stars. Besides stars, many galaxies contain a great deal of **material** in the form of fine dust and gases. Sometimes the light from hot glowing **gas** outshines the stars in a galaxy. Apart from the Milky Way, three other galaxies are **visible** to the naked eye. They are called Andromeda, the large Magellanic Cloud and the small Magellanic Cloud.

3. Synonyms

Trident	harpoon
Feign	fabricate
Kiosk	booth
Staunch	stalwart
Blemish	flaw

Test 40

1. Synonyms

Chaos	havoc
Canine	dog
Sever	cut
Cancel	veto
Allocation	quota

2. Idioms

Cut the mustard	d	a. He's crazy
Go down in flames	e	b. No matter what
He's off his rocker	a	c. You'll make mistakes if you rush something
Haste makes waste	c	d. Do a good job
Come rain or shine	b	e. To fail spectacularly

3. Odd one out

1. dollar — pound — ~~money~~ — euro — yen
2. yacht — ship — canoe — ~~ocean~~ — dinghy
3. lunch — ~~eat~~ — dinner — supper — breakfast
4. ~~arm~~ — liver — kidney — heart — skin
5. cheddar — brie — stilton — ~~cracker~~ — edam

Test 41

1. Antonyms

Veer	straighten
Pompous	humble
Bland	lively
Orthodox	unconventional
Volatile	stable

2. Fill in the missing words

On October 14 1066 a battle was fought that decided the **fate** of England, for by nightfall that day King Harold had been killed, his army defeated and William of Normandy had won a **kingdom**. The battle became known as the Battle of Hastings. William had been preparing to **invade** England all through the summer, for he claimed that he and not King Harold, was the rightful heir of Edward the Confessor. The Battle of Hastings is **depicted** on the Bayeux Tapestry which is a famous piece of **needlework** produced during the time of William the Conqueror.

3. Missing letters

1. muscular
2. cardiovascular
3. oxygen
4. arteries
5. leaves

Test 42

1. Fill in the missing words

The first day of Lent is called Ash Wednesday because in the early days of the Church, sinners did public **penance** on that day by attending services dressed in sack-cloths and having ashes scattered over their heads by the priest. Later the **custom** was extended to the entire congregation. The **ceremony** is still held in a simpler version in the Roman Catholic Church. The ashes are sprinkled with holy water, the **priest** then presses his thumb into the mixture and draws a cross on the forehead of each member of the congregation. The ashes used are **obtained** by burning the palms which were blessed the previous year on Palm Sunday.

2. **Synonyms**

Occult   mystical
Weld   fuse
Marriage   matrimony
Formidable daunting
Dialect   language

3. **Idioms**

Curiosity killed the cat	d	a. They're very alike
Have your head in the clouds	e	b. Hear news of something secret
Get wind of something	b	c. He can't make up his mind
He's sitting on the fence	c	d. Stop asking questions
Like two peas in a pod	a	e. Not be concentrating

Test 43

1. **Antonyms**

Superfluous useful
Simple   complicated
Cloudy   distinct
Modern   obsolete
Submissive resistent

2. **Homophones and Homographs**

1. Listening to my **idol** singing makes me so happy.
2. She could always **refuse** to tell him if he asked her for the details.
3. Katy liked to be busy, she could not stand to be **idle**.
4. He wondered what the **object** was on the side of the road.
5. There was a **tear** in her dress after she caught it on the gate.
6. "I **object** to being spoken to in that way!" he said indignantly.
7. The workmen came to collect the **refuse** on Wednesdays.
8. A **tear** ran down her cheek as she waved goodbye.

3. **Odd one out**

1. kid   puppy   kitten   foal   ~~horse~~
2. yurt   ~~yogurt~~   teepee   wigwam   tent
3. fork   knife   spoon   chopsticks   ~~plate~~
4. dawdle amble   loiter   ~~hurry~~   stroll
5. stem   petal   leaf   ~~tree~~   root

Test 44

1. **Antonyms**

Cursory   detailed
Uniform   disorderly
Capability inability
Covert   candid
Former   latter

2. **Synonyms**

Abhor   detest
Trivial paltry
Juvenile formative
Coax   cajole
Aperture chasm

3. **Idioms**

Let sleeping dogs lie	d	a. Run very fast
Run like the wind	a	b. Both people are responsible
It takes two to tango	b	c. Work quickly, time is a valuable resource
Jump on the bandwagon	e	d. Stop discussing an issue
Time is money	c	e. Follow a trend

Test 45

1. Synonyms

Jingoistic	loyal
Odyssey	excursion
Brood	consider
Swivel	pivot
Wit	satire

2. Homophones and Homographs

1. The prisoner was kept in his **cell** until 4pm.
2. They went for a walk in the **evening** to watch the fireworks.
3. The waves were **evening** out around the boat.
4. The **project** was coming together well and would soon be finished.
5. Sarah tried to **wind** up the toy but feared it might be broken.
6. Colin could feel the **wind** on his face as he ran around the track.
7. Simon tried to **project** the javelin as far as possible to win first place.
8. If I can **sell** 300 per week I can break even.

3. Antonyms

Winsome	displeasing
Spurious	valid
Sobriety	intemperance
Scurrilous	decent
Reprobate	moral

Test 46

1. Antonyms

Grieve	rejoice
Forte	weakness
Apt	unlikely
Appreciate	depreciate
Tame	agitate

2. Fill in the missing words

In the southwest of the United States of America, there is an area of high **tablelands**, deep canyons and rich red sand. This is where the Navaho Indians live. For these **people**, magic is a part of everyday life, just as it was for Stone Age man thousands of years ago. The Navahos use magic in **ceremonies** to bring them rain, to grow their crops, to drive away evil spirits and to cure illness. The magic of Stone Age man was much **simpler**. It began with dances or drawings for **success** when hunting animals for food.

3. Synonyms

Emulate   imitate
Ambiguous   dubious
Dogmatic   fanatical
Restive   jittery
Joust   bout

Test 47

1. Fill in the missing words

Acids are among the most useful and sometimes the most **dangerous** of chemical substances. Hydrochloric acid, for example, is a deadly poison, but if people did not have a small quantity of this acid in their **stomachs** they would not be able to digest their food properly. At one time it was thought that all acids contained **oxygen** but this was found to be incorrect. It is now known that all acids contain **hydrogen**, which is given off when metals are dissolved in an acid. Acids that come from plants or animals are **known** as organic acids.

2. Idioms

Weather the storm	c	a. This isn't over yet
A dime a dozen	d	b. The worse possible situation
Give you the benefit of the doubt	e	c. Go through something difficult
It ain't over till the fat lady sings	a	d. Something common
A perfect storm	b	e. Trust what you say

3. Odd one out

1. screen   keyboard   mouse   motherboard   ~~desk~~
2. boot   ~~shoe~~   bonnet   seats   doors
3. rock   disco   classical   grunge   ~~classic~~
4. sleet   snow   ~~wind~~   hail   rain
5. English   Japanese   ~~France~~ Spanish   Portuguese

Test 48

1.   Fill in the missing words

Thorough **preparation** is the key to successful decorating. If you neglect or **skimp** over the groundwork, the finished surface will always suffer. First, make ready the **area** to be decorated. Indoors, **isolate** the room where you will be working before preparing the surfaces. Most **preparatory** work creates mess and dust which easily spreads to other areas. Wherever possible, clear out everything movable before you start work.

2.   Synonyms

Warden	caretaker
Rebuke	chide
Zeal	diligence
Zenith	apex
Jeer	ridicule

3.   Antonyms

Proscribe	allow
Obdurate	amenable
Nadir	top
Multifarious	homogenous
Largesse	meanness

Test 49

1.   Antonyms

Averse	agreeable
Flout	heed
Reverence	disregard
Envelop	release
Bitter	grateful

2.   Synonyms

Deride	scorn
Endurance	stamina
Axe	cancel
Shrewd	canny
Collaborator	partner

3. Idioms

Add insult to injury	c	a. Very expensive
Costs an arm and a leg	a	b. Tell me what you're thinking
A picture is worth a 1000 words	e	c. To make a bad situation worse
Bite off more than you can chew	d	d. Take on something that you cannot finish
A penny for your thoughts	b	e. Better to show than tell

Test 50

1. Missing letters

1. celebrated
2. coronation
3. victory
4. anniversary
5. regalia
6. festivities

2. Odd one out

1. ash   rowan   ~~burn~~   willow   beech
2. nose   wing   hold   ~~eye~~   tail
3. vast   ~~spread~~ large   huge   immense
4. helium oxygen   ~~tin~~   nitrogen   hydrogen
5. ~~Africa~~ Nigeria Somalia   Chad   Morocco

3. Idioms

Give someone the cold shoulder	b	a. Slow down
Barking up the wrong tree	e	b. To ignore someone
Easy does it	a	c. Don't give up
Hang in there	c	d. Unwell
Under the weather	d	e. To be mistaken

Contact Us

For further information visit our website www.elevenplustutorials.co.uk

Contact or follow us via twitter @plus_tutorials

Contact or follow us via facebook @elevenplustutorials

Free Additional Tests

If you would like five free additional tests please leave a review on amazon and forward a copy of your review by email to elevenplustutorials@gmail.com. Your free tests will be emailed to you by return.

Printed in Great Britain
by Amazon